Monsters of Modernity

Global Icons for our Critical Condition

Julian C. H. Lee, Hariz Halilovich,
Ani Landau-Ward, Peter Phipps,
& Richard J. Sutcliffe

kismet·press

Libera Scientia | Free Knowledge

Monsters of Modernity: Global Icons for our Critical Condition
by Julian C. H. Lee, Hariz Halilovich, Ani Landau-Ward,
Peter Phipps, & Richard J. Sutcliffe

Monsters & Monstrosity, 1
Series Editors: Tim Barnwell & N. Kıvılcım Yavuz

Published in 2019
by Kismet Press LLP
Kismet Press LLP
15 Queen Square, Leeds, LS2 8AJ, UK
kismet.press
kismet@kismet.press

Printed and bound by IngramSpark with acid-free paper, using a print-on-demand model with printers in the US, EU, and Australia

A catalogue record for this book is available from the British Library

ISBN 978-1-912801-04-6 (pbk)
ISBN 978-1-912801-06-0 (hbk)
ISBN 978-1-912801-05-3 (ebk)

Contents

Illustrations

I

Here Be Dragons

THE SEA HAS ALWAYS BEEN A FRIGHTENING PLACE FOR JULIAN, BUT I WAS also drawn to it. When I was younger I would regularly snorkel with friends in the bays around Melbourne. While I never told them so, I dreaded letting them out of my sight. I feared even the most modest of sea animals, including small cuttlefish that browsed the sand and harmless wafting jellyfish. I gave stingrays my fascination and respect.

Being so frightened of the underwater world should have meant I stayed away from the water, and there were those in my family who wished that I would. A great-grandmother of mine issued a mysterious prophecy-of-sorts about my brother and me, that we needed to very careful around water. I could feel the ominousness of the warning around me in the water, just out of sight, like one of the many small swimming creatures I feared and was fascinated by. Even out of the water, when anticipating a new series of David Attenborough's documentaries, it has always been the episodes about the oceans and the rivers that I look forward to the most.

The most memorable creature I ever saw while snorkelling was a leafy sea dragon in Western Port Bay. In cold shallow murky water, I noticed it. I was astonished because I had wrongly thought that they were inhabitants of warm northern waters around the Great Barrier Reef. The leafy sea dragon is a genuinely amazing animal — simultaneously humble and magnificent.

We usually think of dragons as bold, grand creatures. However, dragons are also often portrayed as elusive and hidden, defying detection. They are mysterious and impossible to know, as well as dangerous.

Thus cartographers depicted them on their maps in those parts of the world about which there was no knowledge, which were unknown and therefore perilous. After drawing the known world, notes Simon Best, map makers were 'left with vast unknown spaces on their parchment [on which they] carefully quilled the words "Here be dragons." For these were the places where no-one ventured, or, if they did, never came back, or, if they returned, were never the same again'.[1]

Over time the phrase 'Here be dragons' — *Hic sunt dracones* in Latin — entered popular imagination. However, according to Robinson Meyer, old maps don't in fact carry this phrase. He notes that, 'Old maps—early modern European maps—contain uncharted territory, across which beasts rumble and serpents writhe. They have dragons'.[2] But, he reports, only one globe — the 1510 Hunt-Lenox Globe — contains the phrase *Hic sunt dracones*.[3]

Why, then, is the phrase so much part of our idiom? Meyer concludes that we don't know. Our belief that the phrase is ubiquitous in olde cartography is at odds with reality. But it evidently has a role to play.

Anthropologist Tim Ingold draws on dragons in seeking to 'make a space for art and literature, for religion, or for the beliefs and practices of indigenous peoples, in an economy of knowledge in which the search for the true nature of things has become the exclusive prerogative of rational science'.[4] Dragons and other monsters today are unfeared, Ingold notes, 'as the only people they can eat were as imaginary as themselves'.[5] However, it was not always thus, and this contemporary condition of dragons and mythical beasts as unmenacing has at its heart an oversight.

Ingold tells the story of a monk described in Gregory the Great's *Life of St Benedict of Nursia*, ca. 594 CE. The monk in question seemed to yearn to leave the monastery, and his behaviour caused Benedict to expel him. However, upon stepping outside, the monk was faced with a fearsome dragon. The monk called for help, and the brothers within brought him back inside, although they themselves could observe no dragon. Ingold observes that the brother was not regarded as unhinged or 'hallucinating'. They knew that 'the dragon was not the objective cause of fear; it was the shape of fear itself'.

---

1   Best 1988, 239.
2   Meyer 2013.
3   Cf. Holloway 2017.
4   Ingold 2013, 735.
5   Ibid., 736.

For the brethren of monastic communities, this shape would have been well known to all, drummed in through rigorous discipline of mind and body. In this training, stories and pictures of dragons and of other, equally terrifying monsters were used not as we would today, to create a comfort zone of safety and security by consigning everything that might be frightening to the realms of make-believe, but to instil fear in novices, so that they might experience it, recognize its manifestations, and — through a stern regime of mental and bodily exercise — overcome it. As the manifest form of a fundamental human feeling, the dragon was the palpable incarnation of what it meant to 'know' fear. Thus in medieval ontology, the dragon existed as fear exists, not as an exterior threat but as an affliction instilled at the core of the sufferer's very being.[6]

For Ingold, we are poorer for the absence of monsters in our world, where only those creatures that are classifiable by science may be considered by them. Those unclassified are relegated to science fiction. The journal *Nature*, a pinnacle publisher of science fact, published in 2015 an article that correlated the presence of dragons in social consciousness with increases in global temperature. Through invoking our understanding of dragons, the authors conclude that 'climatic conditions are rapidly reaching an optimum for breeding dragons'.[7] They do this to implicitly call for more to be done to mitigate climate change.

The invocation of dragons, of all monsters, is surely not accidental. Indeed, what the phrase 'Here be dragons' encapsulates may serve as something of a philosophy to guide our understanding of and engagement with the world. 'In our future,' Professor of Quantum Computing David Deutsch has observed, 'the greatest dangers will inevitably be unforeseen'.[8] In a similar vein, Shirin Elahi has noted that while our abilities to know the world are immense, we often overestimate our ability to know. For Elahi, dragons are metaphors for 'the unacknowledged blind spots' that challenge our sense of mastery of the world.[9] But, he asks, shouldn't we abandon the desire for mastery and

6   Ingold 2013, 737.
7   Hamilton, May, and Waters 2015.
8   In RN 2015.
9   Elahi 2011, 196.

instead 'accept the value of "Here be dragons" as a warning signal?'[10] Such warnings have been needed in the many human follies and tragedies caused by overconfidence.

It is easy to bring to mind at this moment that 'the road to hell is paved with good intentions'. But if the road to hell is thusly paved, of what then is the road to heaven made? By deduction: bad intentions? Acting with good intentions is bad? The saying is often recalled when a well-meaning deed leads to misfortune. Julian has often thought that this is well exemplified by Anna's actions in *Anna and the King* (a film adaptation of *The King and I*), where her public outburst intended to save Lady Tuptim from being put to death prevents the King from pardoning her as he intended. To pardon Lady Tuptim after Anna's protests would intolerably suggest to the King's subjects who witnessed it that the King was beholden to Anna, a foreigner and hierarchically inferior.

Another criticism of 'good intentions' that I frequently hear relates to 'voluntourism'. Voluntourists are people who combine a volunteering activity, usually in a development context, with a holiday, and often enabled by a for-profit organisation. The criticisms are several and well founded. These include that volunteers can sometimes cause diverse forms of harm, such as displacing jobs that locals might otherwise be paid for, and that it reinforces global discourses of who is empowered and who is needy.[11] Although Julian has great sympathies with the criticisms, I feel the deployment of 'good intentions' with a pejorative tone, as is so often the case in discussions about voluntourism, overlooks the problem which should actually be focused on. That is, it is not good intentions that pave the road to hell, but ignorance. The problem with Anna's actions was not that she had good intentions, but that she was ignorant of the King's intentions and the cultural context in which she was operating. And the problem with those seeking to undertake voluntourism is not their desire for a better world, but their options and knowledge about how to go about this. In the present context, the critiques of voluntourism should be regarded as part of the conversation about how to fulfil the desires for a better world, but should be done so without throwing the baby of human concern for others with the bathwater of voluntourism's current shortcomings.

In a context where we all must act with varying degrees of ignorance — for we cannot be acquainted with every factor and perspective of relevance — dragons can assist us in being mindful of the dangers of acting in ignorance,

10 Ibid., 197.
11 E.g., McGloin and Georgeou 2015.

as well as arrogance. There is probably no better instance of this in popular culture than Godzilla, a global phenomenon widely interpreted as our way of dealing with humanity's misadventure with nuclear power and its impacts on people and the environment.[12] Speaking of the impending disaster represented in the monsters that emerge in the 2014 Godzilla film, the character Joe Brody cries out to those keeping him captive and who are observing the incubation of one of the monsters, that 'you have no idea what's coming!' And, that 'it is gonna send us back to the Stone Age!'

The destructive power of Godzilla and other giant monsters which could send humanity to the Stone Age provides us with an opportunity to explore through a different lens some global threats facing humanity. These threats are highly complex and multi-causal. The causes and consequences of climate change, for example, do not lend themselves to simple and accurate description, and yet their impacts are increasingly changing the ways we all must live.[13] Ulrich Beck illustrates this with an effective parallel situation regarding responsibility for harm done by lead crystal factories in the 1980s to the town of Altenstadt in former West Germany.

> Flecks of lead and arsenic the size of a penny had fallen on the town, and fluoride vapours had turned leaves brown, etched windows and caused bricks to crumble away. Residents were suffering from skin rashes, nausea and headaches. There was no question where all of that originated. The white dust was pouring visibly from the smokestacks of the factory. A clear case.[14]

And yet the judge dropped the charges and only a modest fine was paid. This was because there were three other similar factories polluting the area. 'Notice,' writes Beck, that 'the more pollution is committed, the less is committed'.[15] How much more so would the case be with a global phenomenon like climate change?

Thus, Beck describes us as living now in a 'risk society'. He writes that 'being at global risk is the human condition at the beginning of the twenty-first century,' and that 'ignorance of the globalization of risk increases the

---

12 TsuTsui 2004.

13 Cf. Kelbert 2016.

14 Beck 1992, 102.

15 Ibid., 103.

globalization of risk'.[16] We are faced with 'mega-hazards'. We are confronted by 'the historically unprecedented possibility of the destruction through decision-making of all life on this planet,' a fact that makes our era different from every other era.[17] Should the 'worst imaginable accident' occur, Beck notes that we won't be able to fix or repair the damage. And furthermore, such an accident would be profound, without 'delimitations in time and space'. 'It becomes an event with a beginning and no end; an "open-ended festival" of creeping, galloping and overlapping waves of destruction'.[18]

Beck's descriptions and reference to 'decision-making' bring to mind most readily nuclear power, weapons, and accidents. Meanwhile, we might be tempted to think of 'natural' disasters as being different to 'man-made' nuclear disasters. However, this shouldn't be the case. Joe Brody, again, provides us an opportunity for considering this through Godzilla. On the same occasion as I quoted him earlier, referring to a fictional Fukushima-like disaster in Japan, he says, 'you're not fooling anybody when you say that what happened fifteen years ago was a natural disaster'.

Although the cause was a monster with which Godzilla later does battle, we can, in reading Godzilla metaphorically as we do in more detail later in this book, extract a wider and important point about the naturalness of natural disasters. Bryan S. Turner and Habibul Haque Khondker, in considering this point, recall Jean-Jacques Rousseau's comments about the 1755 Lisbon earthquake which killed ninety thousand people. Rousseau wrote that 'nature did not construct twenty thousand houses of six to seven stories there, and that, if the inhabitants of this great city had been more equally spread out and more lightly lodged, the damage would have been much less and perhaps of no account'.[19]

In examining the impact of the 2008 earthquake that struck Bam in Iran and which resulted in over eighty thousand fatalities, Roger Musson of the British Geological Survey describes an earlier earthquake that hit a nearby village. It was located between two deserts — the Desert of Salt and the Desert of Death. 'And you would think that was such a terrible coincidence. Given all the uninhabited desert, why did the earthquake have to strike there?' The answer lay in the fact that it was located near freshwater springs. 'But those

16 Beck 2006, 330.
17 Beck 1992, 101.
18 Ibid., 102.
19 Turner and Khondker 2010, 150.

springs were there precisely because the water was coming up along the line of a fault'.[20] And regarding the death toll in Bam, Musson recalls how he had spoken to an engineer who'd visited the town prior to its earthquake and found two bricks which turned to dust when he smacked them together. And so when the earthquake struck Bam, 'the houses were not just destroyed; they turned to dust. So people were simply suffocated in their houses. It's really a horrible thing'.[21]

Turner and Khondker also note that high numbers of casualties have occurred on other occasions when natural and man-made impacts combined. The death toll as a result of an earthquake in China in 2008 was made greater by substandard construction, and the impacts of the 2004 Indian Ocean earthquake and tsunami, also known as the Boxing Day Tsunami, were made worse where mangroves had been removed when creating tourist beaches.[22] Although 'it would be impossible to deny the role of nature in the causation of disasters,' write Turner and Khondker, 'natural causes are mediated by social and political processes and hence we must insert quotation marks around the word "natural"'.[23]

We have sufficient evidence that greater heed must be paid to the consequences of our actions; it is difficult to predict the knock-on effects and adverse outcomes for both people and the environment.[24] How might we better approach the issues facing us in a world that is in a critical condition? We might adopt dragons. These monsters 'turn up apparently independently in a variety of cultures' and so might seem universal.[25] We might adopt them not as an act of hubris and overconfidence, but as a means of troubling our certainties, certainties built upon a global narrative of humanity's command and control of its world — the 'myth of civilisation,' as Paul Kingsnorth describes it. This myth, writes Kingsnorth,

> is built upon the stories we have constructed about our genius, our indestructibility, our manifest destiny as a chosen species. It is where our vision and our self-belief intertwine with our reckless

20 In Copper 2013.

21 Ibid.

22 Turner and Khondker 2010, 150.

23 Ibid.

24 E.g., O'Shaughnessy 2008.

25 Cohen 1990, p. 158.

refusal to face the reality of our position on this Earth. It has led the human race to achieve what it has achieved; and has led the planet into the age of ecocide.[26]

'Here be dragons' calls us to explore that about which we need to know more, and to do so critically; it warns us of the need to proceed carefully in our world of immeasurable complexity and ambiguity. Dragons may be good companions in our thinking. Their magnificence, whether imposing like Godzilla or modest like the leafy sea dragon, should inspire us with awe, and induce in us a humbleness to which we must most urgently become committed.

26 Kingsnorth 2017, 272–73.

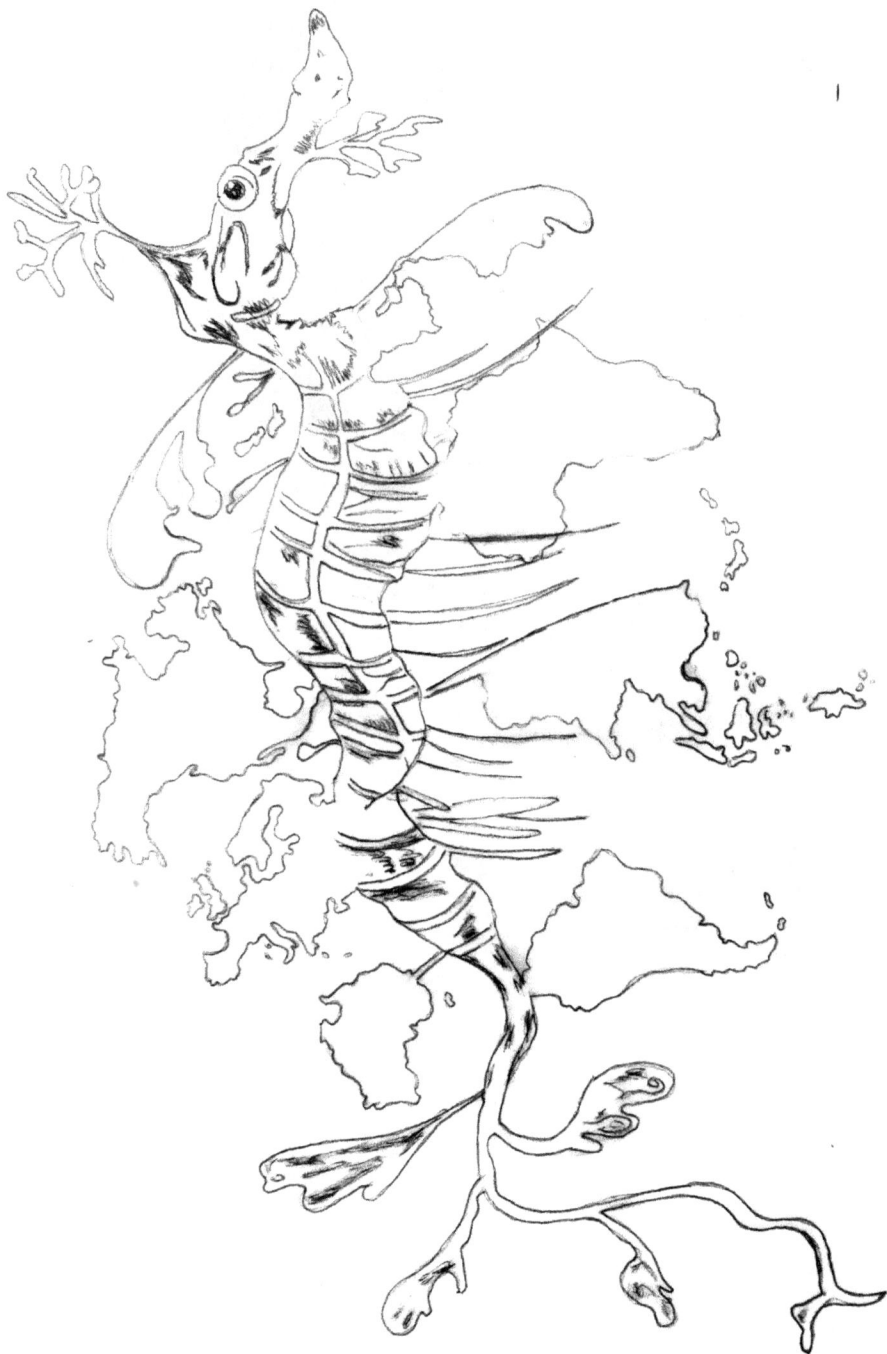

Figure 1. 'Phycodurus eques mundi', by Al Gevers.

Figure 2. 'The sleep of reason produces monsters (El sueño de la razon produce
monstruos)', by Francisco de Goya y Lucientes.

II

The Functional Autonomy of Monsters — A Metalogue

J: Peter, I know you disagree with me about dreams.

P: Remind me, Julian.

J: That the dream is a manifestation of the dreamer's subconscious, or is a way for the dreamer to wrestle with issues they are facing.

P: Oh yes, but why is it relevant in our book about monsters? Are monsters constructions of our imagination and dreams?

J: Not so much that. Okay, to recap our conversation: Do you recall the dream I reported to you where we argued about something work-related and I tried to affirm that I didn't want the argument to affect the friendship?

P: Yes. I suggested that your dream was you coming to terms with a new role you were stepping into at the time — a position which meant that you were going to be in a formally superior position to me at work. I thought this might be making you anxious.

J: And I said that I tended to take a different view of dreams. I felt that dreams contained very little intrinsic meaning. That's not to say they don't have interpretive uses. It is only that the insight that they offer into our selves is through the interpretation we give to it.

P: I understand your view. I'm not sure I entirely agree with it. Actually, I should be more myself and less diplomatic like you and just say 'I don't agree with it'. But carry on.

J: In the chapter on dragons, I noted that the Latin phrase *Hic sunt dracones* occurs only on one known globe, and yet those who know the phrase tend to think it is commonplace on 'olde' maps. The question then arises as to whether it matters that the belief is commonplace, but wrong.

P: Okay. I see where you are going. You're wrangling with possible disconnects between common understanding and 'objective truth'.

J: Right. I couldn't have put it better myself. The issue is relevant to what we are doing in this book because we are discussing monsters and what different monsters *mean* and how they reflect an array of issues and concerns that are the result of humanity's trajectories and aspirations toward, or entry into, modernity, however one might wish to define the era or condition. But I'm hesitant to have us make claims about what a given monster should 'objectively' be regarded as meaning, as opposed to what we take it to mean. I'm loath to make claims about any 'objective' meaning of a monster — whether somehow inherently or even for a collectivity of people. Even though I'm half Malaysian-Chinese, I don't think I want to make claims about what dragons mean for Chinese or Malaysian-Chinese people.

P: So, then, is this book just about 'What this monster means to me?'

J: I see what you're saying. I don't want it to be so *entirely* subjective. I need help to work this out.

P: Okay. Tell me when you last encountered a monster. Let's go with dragons.

J: A real dragon, other than a leafy sea dragon? Never, of course.

P: So how do you know about dragons?

J: From everything I've read, seen, heard, watched.

P: Was everything you read, saw, heard, and watched created by you?

J: No.

P: Perhaps then you can say, and we can say, that our interpretations of monsters are not unmoored from the societies that created them. They remain entangled in cultural 'webs of meaning', even though some monsters are taken across significant physical and cultural distances to new places where their meaning and significance evolves. Our monsters are of human worlds and minds. They are not just of the minds of the authors of this book.

J: Right. Even if we wanted to, I don't think we could create a wholly subjective and idiomatic interpretation of a monster.

P: Julian, I don't think we need to be excessively worried about being thought of as too idiosyncratic. But the point you're trying to make is important. Tell me though, what is it?

J: That what we are doing is not seeking to give some 'objective' account of what a monster is or means, but that we are dealing with interpretations — both our interpretations and the interpretations of others, and sometimes more one than the other. This is something that Richard will have more to say about in the next chapter, and quite comprehensively I'm sure. But this all brings me to where I started. In the same way as I tend not to be interested in the intrinsic meaning of dreams, I'm not supposing that we will make claims about the intrinsic meanings of our monsters. What will be more revealing are the interpretations of those monsters, and *what those monsters are taken to mean.*

P: If that is the case, you are — we are! — letting monsters loose!

J: And I think I have grounds for this. Many years back I was taken by a concept of the psychologist Gordon Allport — the functional autonomy of motives. In short, he argued that our motives as adults, although founded in childhood, are functionally independent of those roots. I have here a quote of his from 1937:

> Just as a child gradually repudiates his dependence on his parents, develops a will of his own, becomes self-active and self-determining, and outlives his parents, so it is with motives. Each motive has a definite point of origin which may possibly lie in instincts, or, more likely, in the organic tensions of infancy. Chronologically speaking, all adult purposes can be traced back to these seed-forms in infancy, but as the individual matures the tie is broken. Whatever bond remains, is historical, not functional.[1]

The point made here is for me essential. I don't feel our discussions of monsters *need* to somehow address the roots of our monsters or to make assertions about their deep or inherent or intrinsic meanings. Monsters are connected to but can be functionally autonomous of those origins...

P: The functional autonomy of monsters...

J: ...and their meaning is to be understood in the now. Allport wrote that 'Motives being always contemporary should be studied in their present structure'. Replace 'motives' with 'monsters'.

P: We can find monsters in their habitats, and then take them for a walk.

J: And to see where they go and what they do. But given that they have a form, known behaviours, and that there are patterns in the way people talk about and react to them, it isn't that our monsters are *completely* free.

---

1   Allport 1937.

P: No, but they invite us to think about and through certain things in certain ways. Different monsters will lend themselves to addressing different elements of our human condition.

J: Right, and I think there's benefit in that. Mary Catherine Bateson in *Angels Fear* said much the same, but with respect to people. If you have a few more moments, I'll quote the paragraph.

P: I can't stop you.

J: [...] one can use an imagined identification with another person to enhance one's understanding of an idea or event by asking, how would so-and-so see this? The mental model of another personality [...] can introduce some novelty [...], thinking oneself into the other person — and one can do this repeatedly, playing a question through alternate filters and seeing how it is processed each time. The same thing can be done with a group, a number of people whose interactions as well as their individual styles and voices are familiar, members of a conference, say, or a committee. For a time I used my memory of the Wenner-Gren Conference in 1968 in this way, asking, can I hear Gertrude discussing that? Or Tolly? And, of course, I have done it repeatedly in working on this book. How would Gregory respond to that? The names even become verbs in mental shorthand: Can I 'Gregory' this idea? This methodology made this writing feel like a series of new encounters, as I met my father saying new things. One of the most basic forms of meditation in the Christian tradition has been the effort to imagine oneself (and the dilemmas presented by one's life) into the person of Jesus, *Imitatio Christi*, and other traditions propose related kinds of identification.[2]

I think what I see us doing in this book is something similar with monsters. We are using them as vehicles to explore, and think things through. And sometimes, perhaps, *Imitatio Monstra*.

P: Julian, there's a question I've been wanting to ask, but I sense I know the answer. Why am I talking like you, and using the kinds of turns of phrase that you do? It's because I'm not really writing any of this, am I? Your dialogue and mine are both written by you. This is why I couldn't stop you quoting Bateson.

2   Bateson and Bateson 1979, 194.

J: Yes, Peter.

P: But why me, and not any of the other authors?

J: Because the issue I've been trying to think through here seemed to me, in essence, the same one we were dealing with in that discussion in my office about the dream I had. In trying to work out how we were writing about monsters, I kept going back to that conversation. You came to represent a particular position, which I constructed in my mind as an opposing position to my own, and which I was seeking to engage with. The means by which I tried to resolve it was by talking it through with my imagined Peter, and what he represented. What I'm not sure of is how the 'real' Peter would react. But I don't know if that matters.

Figure 3. 'The Chimera (La Chimère de Monsieur Desprez)', by Louis Jean Desprez.

III

Polymorphous Monstrosity: Some Chimerical Reflections on the Question — What Is a Monster?

Belief in monsters was common throughout the pre-modern world, and continues [...] today. Their importance, their significance, extends well beyond the base question of their reality, though. Whether we believe or disbelieve the existence of a phenomenon is not what grants it social and cultural force. The question is not therefore 'Did people believe in monsters?'—they did, and still do—but rather, 'What is a monster?'[1]

The Monster Mash

Things happened that later millennia found it hard to understand. A head came without a body. Two heads arrived, one behind the other. A single hind leg chose its body, which already had four legs. Six antlers settled in a single skull.[2]

Because this wasn't the monster he was expecting.[3]

---

1   Mittman 2016, 6.
2   Berger 1996.
3   Ness 2012, 21.

I, Richard, assemble a text here that is itself monstrous, comprised partly of fragments of other texts about monsters. I am responding as a bricoleur to my question: What is a monster? Or, rather, I want to ask: What are monsters?

While my co-authors explore particular monsters, I conduct my bricolage in the spirit of the popular online children's game 'Mix a Monster', which invites players to 'combine ingredients in the magic cauldron to create terrifying monsters'. I am in pursuit of insight into the general problem of *what monsters are*.

However, reformulating my question from What is a monster? to What are monsters? presents a somewhat different problem, i.e., the multiplicity of monsters (or of representations of monsters) and the question of whether they share commonalities (or perhaps 'family resemblances'). Nevertheless, this is clearly not intended to be an exhaustive or even comprehensive study; I am merely sketching some ideas. Although I will mention a range of different monsters, the primary focus here is on the hermeneutics *of* monsters, i.e., interpretations of monsters. More specifically, then, the problem being explored is: What have 'monsters' been taken to be? So instead of asking 'What might this particular monster mean?' or taking a monster 'for a walk' as my co-authors do, I am asking 'What has been meant by monsters?' This chapter therefore picks up and expands threads in the metalogue between Julian and an imagined Peter. To acquire greater purchase on my questions, proliferating like hydra, I will need to 'look' at some monsters, and the domains in which they can be found, and also consider what is said about them. But not necessarily in that order. I roam *wildly*.

The move from specific monsters to monsters-in-general is appropriate at least in the sense that the term 'monster' can be used in a generic way as a category that includes various disparate and more particular forms of creatures that are also known and described *as* monsters (e.g., dragons, werewolves, aliens, demons, giants, vampires, the Manticore). Beyond this very diversity of monsters, though, I suggest that the category of monster is *itself* intrinsically amorphous and unstable. Whereas particular monsters, like dragons, will usually have several more or less *conventional* features — breathing fire, wings, guarding treasure, etc. — that form an ensemble enabling us to recognise them as dragons, this is less clearly the case for monsters taken 'as a whole'. Asma has suggested that from the point of view of cognitive linguistics, the term and concept of monster functions as a prototype category.[4] This means that

---

4 Asma 2009, 282.

it is unlikely that we can find a single way of defining monsters that would be able to include all possible monsters. Indeed, in the epilogue to *Monsters: An Unnatural History of Our Worst Fears*, Asma notes that, 'one will search in vain through this book to find a single compelling definition of *monster*. That's not because I forgot to include one, but because I don't think there is one'.[5] We should perhaps take this as a demonstrative warning, in the ominous sense of *monstrum*, to which I will soon turn.

Metamorphic Monstrosity: What Has 'Monster' Meant?

A whole mythology is deposited in our language.[6]

In everything there is something monstrous that we have to keep quiet about.[7]

Divining with Monsters

Every one, as he returned from some far-distant region, told of wonders, of violent hurricanes, and unknown birds, of monsters of the sea, of forms half-human, half beast-like, things they had really seen or in their terror believed.[8]

In the *Pharsalia*, an uncompleted epic poem by the Roman poet Lucan (39–65 CE), we find the following passage: 'He knows thoroughly the course of the thunderbolt, the marks on entrails still warm and the messages of winged creatures that fly through the air. He orders […] the destruction of monsters which nature had produced, as abnormal births from mixed seed and gives instructions to burn the abominable offspring of a barren womb with wood from a tree of bad omen'.[9] Lucan is describing Arruns, an Etruscan *haruspex*. *Haruspices* were diviners who read the entrails of sacrificial victims, practitioners of the *Estrusca disciplina* (the 'Etruscan art'), or *haruspicina*. In

---

5 Ibid., 281–82.
6 Wittgenstein 1979, 10e.
7 Benjamin 2004, 16.
8 Tacitus, *Annals* 2.24 1986, 29.
9 *Phars.* 1.584ff., cited in Luck 1987, 252.

ancient Rome, the *haruspices* formed an institution that rivalled the *augures* (diviners who interpreted the sound, flight, and feeding patterns of birds).[10] In Lucan's narrative, Arruns performs a sacrifice and foresees a disaster (the impending civil war between Caesar and Pompey), but does not have the courage to speak the truth of what he sees.

Monsters appear here in the context of *cosmopolitical* divination with entrails. The Romans had taken up *haruspicina* from the Etruscans, who had brought it from the Near East, since 'we know that it was practiced by the Babylonians and the Hittites'.[11] This form of divination was one of an enormous repertoire of techniques (dream interpretation, oracular institutions, etc.) known in antiquity, many of which derived from Mesopotamia.[12] Here we are dealing with traces of social imaginary significations reaching back five millennia or so in human civilizational history. Anthropologist David Gilmore, in his *Monsters: Evil Beings, Mythical Beasts, and All Manner of Imaginary Terrors*, argues that it is here that we first find monsters: 'Aside from some equivocal figures in European cave art [...] the first unequivocal and identifiable monsters are to be found in early dynastic Egypt and Mesopotamia, and possibly a little later in the Indus Valley in present-day Pakistan. Indeed monsters arise with civilization — with human self-consciousness'.[13]

According to Luck, Lucan's text furnishes us with an important clue in interpreting *monstra*, i.e., 'unnatural things or events in nature'. These include 'teratological, that is, abnormal or monstrous, formations in animals or plants, misshapen organisms of any kind, and strange meteorological phenomena. Such events were reported from all parts of Italy, to be analysed by experts, and if they occurred more frequently in one particular year, rumors of an impending crisis began to circulate'.[14] Lucan's poem also tells us that the *haruspex* could 'order the destruction of monsters'. This relates to the practice of infanticide. Under Roman law, a father was required to 'immediately put to death a son recently born, who is a monster, or has a form different from that of the members of the human race'.[15] This is the first ingredient in our 'Mix a Monster' cauldron.

---

10 Cf. Ogilvie 2000, 64–67.
11 Luck 1987, 251.
12 Cf. Leick 2002, 235ff.
13 Gilmore 2002, 5.
14 Luck 1987, 252; cf. Ogilvie 2000, 53–69.
15 From *The Twelve Tables*, cited in Asma 2009, 9; cf. Berger 1991, 500.

We see then that the divinatory dimension of monsters is ancient, reaching back to the thresholds of 'recorded history'. But we also see traces of the transmission of symbolic constellations across thousands of years. In what I think is a fascinating survey of the history of teratology, Barrow[16] remarks that the 'Babylonian belief that the future was foretold by the stars, that abnormal infants were reflections of stellar constellations, and hence presaged the future since they indicated the star's positions, was carried into the Greek and Roman civilizations. Thus the Latin word *monstrum* [...] is derived from this concept of a monster's property of foretelling the future'.[17] Monsters were still understood in this way in early modern Europe (e.g., in Luther's religious polemics).[18] Park and Daston have summarised the traditional associations that monsters had in the European context up to the early sixteenth century: 'Characteristically, monsters appear most frequently in the context of a whole group of related natural phenomena: earthquakes, floods, volcanic eruptions, celestial apparitions, and rains of blood, stones and other miscellanea. The interpretation of this canon of phenomena underwent a series of metamorphoses after 1500'.[19]

In short, there is an extensive continuity of ideas about monstrous births (including human cases) as significations or cosmic portents that extends from at least the first millennium BCE, through later antiquity and the medieval era, and well into the early modern and even modern period. Asma writes that 'the Ancients interpreted monsters as omens or signs [...] Monsters continued to function as portents throughout the medieval era and well into the modern'.[20]

Speaking the Language of Monsters

> Metamorphic monstrosity represents the uncanny productivity of linguistic reproduction, an illicit fornication in the basement brothel of the verbal imagination always breeding new figures.[21]

16 Barrow 1971.
17 Ibid., 118.
18 Cf. Park and Daston 1981; Platt 1999.
19 Park and Daston 1981, 23.
20 Asma 2009, 141.
21 Clarke 1995, 84.

> What is a Monster? In contemporary fiction, a monster will inevitably be post-Marxist, post-Freudian/post-Jungian, post-Cinema, post- or maybe merely mid-genetic manipulation. Which, let's face it, isn't very scary.[22]

Our second ingredient is etymological. The English noun 'monster', for which the *OED* provides about five distinct meanings, comes from the Latin word *monstrum*, meaning a) portent, marvel; and b) monster. *Monstra* (plural) were considered omens because 'the appearance of strange and sinister creatures was thought to herald unusual and disturbing events'.[23] One of the possible roots of *monstrum* is *moneo*, meaning to warn or foretell (another is *monstro/monstrare* meaning to show or instruct). We shouldn't forget, though, that ancient Romans also made use of several other words with a similar range of meanings that cluster around the senses of omen, unnatural, marvel, and monster, e.g., *prodigium* (portent; unnatural deed; monster), and *portentum* (omen, unnatural happening; monstrosity, monster; marvel). In addition to this broadly divinatory vocabulary, Latin speakers could make use of *belua* (beast, monster [especially large and fierce]; any animal; brute [figuratively transferred to persons]) and *bestia* (beast, animal without reason). *Bestia* was opposed to *homo* (humans), often literally, implying particularly the animals used in the bloody gladiatorial spectacles. Fittingly, perhaps, the Romans even had an adjective, *beluosus*, used to describe something that was 'full of monsters'.

As with most words, of course, the meanings of 'monster' (in English) have changed over time. Furthermore, its semantic range has expanded. When (Middle) English speakers began using 'monster' (*ca.* the twelfth to fourteenth centuries), adopting it from the French (*monstre* and *mostre*), the word did not have any of the meanings that inform the ways it is predominantly used now. Usage of the Latin, French, and English terms overlapped for a substantial period, all having the same basic meaning of the Latin *monstrum* as an ominous portent. But as the meanings of the word changed, and new senses developed, others become obsolete or more deeply sedimented (and, we might even say, repressed).

---

22 Litt 2016, 196.
23 Miller 1974.

I can now take note of the basic senses of monster in terms of the semantic history provided by the (Shorter) *OED*.[24] In the thirteenth to fourteenth centuries, 'monster' referred to 'a malformed animal or plant; a misshapen birth, an abortion'. However, this was quickly supplemented by the inclusion of fabulous creatures known from myths: 'An imaginary animal, either partly brute and partly human, or compounded of elements from two or more animal forms' (e.g., centaur, sphinx, minotaur). An early example of this use is Chaucer's 'This Mynos hadde a monstre, a wiked best' (i.e., the Minotaur) in his *The Legend of Good Women* (*ca.* 1385). The adjective 'monstrous' is first recorded in 1460. In the sixteenth century two further usages of monster emerge, one involving a reference to size ('An animal of huge size; hence anything of vast proportions', 1530), and the other a metaphoric transference to human behaviour ('A person of inhuman cruelty or wickedness; a monstrous example of (some particular vice)', 1556). 'Monstrosity' is first recorded in 1555. By 1605 'monster' could also be used as a verb (making something/someone a monster by exhibiting them as such). By the early eighteenth century the use of monster to refer to something extraordinary or unnatural ('a prodigy or marvel') developed, returning in a way to the Latin roots of the term, but only adding a well-established early modern usage to the English word. During the nineteenth century monster also came to be used as an adjective (e.g., 'monster meeting') denoting something of 'extraordinary size; gigantic, huge, monstrous'. Provisionally, the core senses of monster in historical semantic terms are then: prodigy, deformed creature, imaginary beast, gigantic entity, cruel person. In our book, we dwell on monsters of all these different types. However, in ordinary language terms, monsters can be creatures both human and non-human (or both), 'real' or 'imaginary', often of large proportions (size, capacity for vice, etc.), and may be understood as marvellous or portentous. As a concept, then, monster is a constellation of several partly overlapping yet also conflicting meanings.

More generally, we find also that some things (entities, beings, creatures, people, etc.) that used to be considered as monsters are no longer included in the 'set', or perhaps receive new labels (e.g., 'freak', 'mutant'), while new monsters are continually being added. Overall, this can have the apparent effect of evacuating the term of consistent meaning. But at the same time, the ongoing incorporation of new monsters also gives different nuances and inflections to the word's semantic range. There is a dynamic tension between

---

24 Cf. Bowman 1999.

a core constellation of sedimented, conventional usages of the term and the expanding semantic field potentially demanded by the inclusion of more and more diverse monsters.

In modern vernacular usage, monster can mean any of the five senses provided by the *OED*. However, there has been a decline in the use of 'monster' to refer to human beings born with physical deformities. In our book, Hariz speaks to the question of human monsters in a following chapter. Meanwhile, arguably the most frequent usages today combine the idea of monster as a fabulous creature, often of composite form, with the idea of an animal of huge size or something of vast proportions. The broad contemporary usage of the term, however, in conjunction with the immense popularity of some mass cultural monsters, has led some scholars to remark that 'our current conception of monster is out of whack'.[25] This calling into question of the capacious ways we use 'monster' today carries with it possible implications. Perhaps we shouldn't like our monsters too much? Or, maybe when we're liking our monsters they're not really monstrous?

Foresman and Tobienne argue that 'being a monster implies being something unpleasant, repulsive, and very scary, which means you literally cannot like it. If you do, then it's not really a monster to you'.[26] While there is an important point being made here, which also opens onto questions about the ways that monsters are domesticated for mass consumption, as explored later in our book in relation to Pokémon, this is perhaps to dismiss too quickly an important part of the enduring *fascination* with monsters, i.e., their sometimes seductive allure. A dynamic of attraction (desire) and repulsion (fear) often inflects human–monster relationships.[27] We are frequently drawn to them in spite of their dangers. They can enchant us with their powers.

On Bringing Monsters to Mind (Or, Don't Think of a Monster!)

The blink of an eye takes roughly 84 milliseconds. Within half that time, according to studies of perceptual illusions and false

---

25 Foresman and Tobienne 2013, 17.
26 Foresman and Tobienne 2013, 16.
27 Cf. Franzen 2007; Fisher 2016, 17; Jones 2018, 42.

memories, you can tap the darkness within and conjure monsters for yourself.[28]

Any terror put into an accomplished enough artistic form becomes enjoyable, and so self-contradictory.[29]

Now that we have a sense of certain early historical contexts from which Western ideas about monsters have derived, as well as the layered meaning-structures of 'monster' in English, we can think about where else monsters might be found.

When I began to think about monsters, to think about them in a way that seeks to arrive at some preliminary conclusions about what they are, or have been, or perhaps may yet become — to think *with* monsters! — I was assailed. I was assailed by a vast array of suggestive possibilities. They crowded my imaginary clearing, from which I wanted to begin my thinking with monsters. Monsters seem to break into this clearing and they beset me from all sides at once. I can imagine monsters on land, sea monsters, monsters coming from the sky (or from 'outer space'), and subterranean monsters. (An evocative illustration here might be Goya's famous etching, *El sueño de la razón produce monstruos* [*The Sleep of Reason Produces Monsters*], completed in 1799, in which bats and owls crowd in upon the sleeping human figure while a lynx looks on. As our eyes take in the movement of the winged creatures they may be drawn into the image's compositional centre. Here, a wolf-like creature looks directly out at the viewer, its gaze drawing them into the image's vortex of forces. For my purposes, the image stands as a conjuration of the phantasmatic proliferation of monsters in the unbridled play of the oneiric imaginary).

Through free association or imaginative variation, figures from Mesopotamian and Mayan cosmology jostle here alongside remembered images from Hollywood B-movies; childhood memories; images of historical inter-human atrocities; extra-terrestrial creatures; serpents in Scottish lochs; wild, hairy, giant anthropoids living in marginal, wooded country; the demonology of various religious traditions; serial killers; vampires and werewolves; amorphous fears of the unknown; humans born with physical deformities (one of the skeletons in the closet of the history of monsters); the dark play of the dreaming world of nightmares; and the psycho-somatic

28 Slater 2014.
29 Eagleton 1999.

constellation of impulses, desires, images, words, and thoughts that fill the ongoing experience of human consciousness with its temperamental shadings of anxiety, hope, passion, fear, etc.

Even if I could not imagine such monsters through a more or less controlled attending to the ongoing intrapsychic flow of imaginary significations, or daydreaming, or some other mode of dissociative reverie, each of these domains (land, sea, sky, chthonic) is readily populated with images drawn from my own experience of popular culture, mass media, genres and subgenres of fiction (e.g., Gothic, sci-fi, horror, fantasy, dark fantasy, weird, children's books), folklore and fairy tales, mythology, and science. Furthermore, as the author of *A Dictionary of Monsters and Mysterious Beasts* suggests to readers: 'If you can't find a monster blood-curdling enough for your taste you can always make one up; you won't be the first person to do it'.[30] But monsters do not always come into our experience through the voluntary direction of wakeful consciousness and reveries of the imagination. As Goya's etching suggests, and as we may know from experience, they can break in from other dimensionalities.

Don't think of a monster!

What sort of monster did you imagine? Was it the monster you had been expecting? Perhaps there was more than one? What sort of figures might we expect to find gathered together under the rubric of monster? This last is by no means a straightforward question. 'The monstrous is a genus too large to be encapsulated in any conceptual system' writes Cohen.[31] *Monster*, as Asma points out, 'is a flexible, multiuse concept'.[32] Let us take a closer look.

We need a first image of some monsters to begin with, so I will take a shortcut here via the fields of literary, popular cultural, and global folkloric monsters. We will look at a *recent* fictional monster, and then make note of some *well-known* pop cultural monsters. We will then select a monster from Hill and Lawrence's *The Atlas of Monsters*.[33] My selections here are more or less arbitrary. We can find a recent literary description of a monster in Patrick Ness's *A Monster Calls* (2012):

30 Miller 1974, 3.
31 Cohen 1996, 7.
32 Asma 2009, 7.
33 Hill and Lawrence 2017.

And yet here was a monster, clear as the clearest night, towering ten or fifteen meters above him, breathing heavily in the night air [...] Every time the monster moved, Conor could hear the creak of wood, groaning and yawning in the monster's huge body. He could see, too, the power in the monster's arms, great wiry ropes of branches constantly twisting and shifting together in what must have been tree muscle, connected to a massive trunk of a chest, topped by a head and teeth that could chomp him down in one bite [...] The monster seemed to grow before Conor's eyes, getting taller and broader. A sudden, hard wind swirled up around them, and the monster spread its arms out wide, so wide they seemed to reach to opposite horizons, so wide they seemed big enough to encompass the world.[34]

We will not dwell on this passage, allowing it rather to take shape in the reader's imagination.

[   ]

But we can notice that this monster is large and powerful, can move with elemental force and rapidly change form and/or size. Like the *Ents* of Tolkien's Middle Earth or perhaps the Slavic *Leshy*, the monster also combines aspects of humanoid and arboreal physiognomy. This composite form is evoked through an emphasis on the monster's *body*. The monster embodies a mixture of two forms of life that — in classificatory terms — are normally distinguished. In other words, although this monster is explicitly *called* a monster, we can also recognise it *as* a monster owing to its conformity to certain conventions associated with representations *of* monsters, *assuming we know these conventions*.

Now, turning to modern popular culture for a moment, in the mass mediated forms produced by global capitalism, let us consider a short catalogue of 'iconic monsters' taken from the internet. This is entitled 'Origins of 10 of the most iconic monsters from pop culture'.[35] Phillipp discusses a 'core group of classic monsters', *viz.*, mummies, Frankenstein, ghouls, vampires, the devil, the boogeyman, zombies, werewolves, witches, and the gillman (a.k.a.

34 Ness 2012, 48–49.
35 Phillipp 2016.

Creature from the Black Lagoon). In passing, we can perhaps underline the dominance of early twentieth-century classic Hollywood cinema in shaping the iconic versions of pop cultural monsters that are now familiar in mass media culture, and behind that, notice a number of tropes already familiar from European Gothic-Romantic literature of the eighteenth and nineteenth centuries (e.g., Frankenstein's monster, vampires). Behind this we can see the Counter-Enlightenment strand of modern culture that is the source for the Romantic Gothic movement which, in turn, has provided the central pattern of conventions for modern monster representations.[36]

These monsters are familiar to us mainly from two dominant mass media forms of the nineteenth and twentieth centuries (*viz.*, the novel, the film). I present them here simply to provide an orientation point regarding pop cultural monsters — a conjuring of monsters from widely distributed forms of mass cultural production and consumption.[37] While other monsters could be added such as King Kong and the Xenomorph Alien discussed in Chapter 6, and the list extended indefinitely, they indicate well enough for our purposes some of the familiar monsters of modern media ecologies that someone exposed to twentieth- and early twenty-first-century popular culture might conceivably 'bring to mind'.[38] These are the monsters of choice for capitalist modernity and the entertainment of its denizens.

Moving now to *The Atlas of Monsters*, which has a global folkloric focus, and selecting a single monster (which means overlooking 222 others, including the Cheese Goblins of the Netherlands) we turn to the pages on South American monsters. Here we find an entry on *Madremonte*: 'This raging spirit of Mother Mountain fiercely protects her land and creatures. Dressed in moss and leaves, she has eyes of fire, sharp fangs and consuming anger for any that would defile her natural world. She is found in Columbia'.[39] This monster is usually interpreted as a guardian of the wild or natural world. Characteristically, she protects the creatures of the jungle, causes wild storms and flooding, and haunts those who steal land. Those who encroach into her domain find themselves confronted by insurmountable obstacles: pathways change direction, become overgrown with vegetation, and even mountains

36 Cf. Allison 2014; Steven 2017, 39; Jones 2018..

37 Cf. Backe 2014.

38 Cf. Sontag 1965; Halberstam 1995; Warner 2007; Hanich 2011.

39 Hill and Lawrence 2017, 51.

transform their shapes. Overcome by dizziness, her victims may fall into a lengthy sleep.

We can already see, then, that a repertoire of monsters can emerge from two distinct but intersecting fields, i.e., the intrapsychic flow of internal imagery and the field of more or less shared cultural-symbolic forms (or the cultural imaginary). In other words, we can find monsters in both the psyche and society. Arguably, we can also find them in 'nature'. Beyond this, from the inner horizons of certain visions of the cosmos, some monsters are *super*natural. Here though, and unlike many recent commentators on monsters, we will not be using 'supernatural' (in the modern vernacular sense) as a general category for describing monsters. For one thing, it is rationally overdetermined. Monsters are not easily constrained within the boundaries of reason alone. (Note, furthermore, that we are not concerned here with the absolute ontology of monsters from a pre-given philosophical position, e.g., 'speculative realism', but with the ways they are given to us in experience and the meanings that we give to them). Phenomenologically, a more useful notion is Harpur's formulation 'daimonic reality', which he applies to the interpretation of visions and apparitions.[40] This concept grants constitutive autonomy to the imagination and evokes a kind of 'third space' in which conventional distinctions between subject and object are blurred. A (transitional) zone of manifestation in which subjects become objects and vice versa is precisely the sort of region from which monsters emerge (e.g., the Caribbean sorcerers known in Trinidad as *legarou* can change themselves into animals, trees, or objects).[41] Grotstein,[42] who has explored the potential movement of monsters across the psyche–world boundary from a psychoanalytic perspective, also points to a transitional zone of experience, developing in human infancy, in which demonic 'third forms' emerge. He suggests that 'In all probability the phantoms, ghosts, monsters, and *chimerae* that occupy and haunt our internal world are part of our inherent template of possibilities and at the same time are created anew from the raw clay of our autochthonous creative projective identifications'.[43] There seems little difficulty in conjuring monsters — be they speculative or otherwise — on either side of the conventional divides between

40 Harpur 1995.
41 See Hill and Lawrence 2017, 48.
42 Grotstein 1997.
43 Ibid., 55.

subject/object and fantasy/reality (and with due reservations about the neatness of these divides in lived human experience).

Although I can only mention this in passing, in historical terms it is possible to discern at least five distinctive strands within Occidental traditions about monsters that have come to inform our monster traditions today. These are: 1) myth (fabulous beasts); 2) cosmographic/ethnographic (fabulous geography, monstrous races, marvels, and wonders); 3) divinatory; 4) juridico-medical; and 5) folkloric/popular cultural. It would be instructive to map these historical discourses against the various meanings of 'monster' considered above, but this task must be reserved for another occasion.

'Ultimately, I myself was this sea animal' (Or, Nietzsche's Lizards and Hegel's Squid)[44]

> The art that distinguishes it is not inconsiderable when it comes to fixing to some extent things that easily flit by, noiselessly — moments I call divine lizards.[45]

> I am a brother to dragons, and a companion to owls.[46]

Monsters are
        dynamic
                            forms.
        They
move
                    around.

We find the serpentine *Nagas*, for example, in India, Thailand, and Indonesia. Monsters leave material traces of the historical and geographical 'migration of symbols'[47] and cognitive-affective traces in the 'cultural memory'[48] of human societies. But in thinking with and about monsters, and where they might come from, the boundaries between the cultural and the biological

44 Nietzsche 1989, 290.
45 Ibid., 291.
46 Job 30:29 (KJV).
47 Wittgower 1942.
48 Assmann 2011.

rapidly become indistinct; likewise, those between the human and the animal domains. Not unusually, in fact, monsters confound conventional categories within classificatory systems; 'the monster's very existence is a rebuke to boundary and enclosure'.[49] In this sense they constitute and/or signify threats to the hegemonic symbolic order.[50] Here we might think of the monstrous wolf of Norse mythology, Fenrir (son of the trickster god Loki), who is prophesied to kill the god Odin during the events of *Ragnarök*. In *Religion and its Monsters*, Beal suggests that monsters 'are threatening figures of anomaly within the well-established and accepted order of things'.[51] Gilmore contends that '[the monster] embodies the existential threat to social life, the chaos, atavism, and negativism that symbolize destructiveness and all other obstacles to order and progress'.[52] Characteristically, monsters inhabit the borderlands and thresholds between different domains (e.g., Cerberus). Or they may mark the frontiers of 'wilderness' and 'civilization' (e.g., *Madremonte*). For Milburn, these 'denizens of the borderland' have 'always represented the extremities of transgression and the limits of the order of things'.[53]

Now, if I *had* to identify a *single* notion that is at the heart of the human experience of monsters, *and* which is also a *ubiquitous* theme in monster hermeneutics, this would be, quite simply, fear (complicated by desire). Whatever else they are taken to be, monsters frighten us. Gilmore suggests that 'monsters embody all that is dangerous and horrible in the human imagination'.[54] They are threatening figures that we fear. The significance of fear in both the direct experience and secondary interpretation of monsters is also clear from Beville's observation that, 'the classification of monsters into various types has long been an exercise in which the types reflect more about specific human fears than they do about the monster itself. These fears are always bound to cultural context and so particular types of monsters remain specific to certain cultural and geographical regions'.[55]

We fear monsters because they embody uncontrollable forces that threaten us. They threaten us by their potential for disordering our attempts to organise

49 Cohen 1995, 7.

50 Cf. Bailey 2008.

51 Beal 2002, 4.

52 As cited in Bailey 2008, 9.

53 Milburn 2003, 603.

54 Gilmore 2002, 1.

55 Beville 2014, 7.

our experience and our lives. From a cognitive-symbolic anthropological perspective, we might suggest, monsters help us to signify chaos to ourselves and, in so doing, they are negative markers of the boundaries of normative forms of order. In fact, even the friendliest of friendly monsters, on closer inspection, may have aspects that are disturbing or anomalous (the Cookie Monster's *appetite*, for example). What we do with our monsters is suggestive, then, of both how we give form to that which we fear, and also of the uses that we find for our fears. Something of this is captured, I think, by author Mike Carey, in the graphic novel *The Unwritten, Volume 1: Tommy Taylor and the Bogus Identity*, when he writes that 'we make our own monsters, then fear them for what they show us about ourselves'.[56]

Creatures of excess, monsters threaten to disturb various dimensions in which more or less normative forms of order are assumed to hold sway, e.g., 'cosmological', 'psychological', 'social', 'natural', or 'ecological' orders. They may lie dormant for long periods of time but then awaken suddenly, and they can move rapidly in from the peripheries towards various centres, demanding our attention, provoking us to respond. Monsters present challenges to our attempts to order the world coherently through their very potency as forces of destruction and dissolution. They are, we might say, 'm o v e r s and s^{h}a$_k$e^{r}s'.

We also see that while contemporary mass culture contains a menagerie of monsters that people eagerly consume, monsters are not only found here. Asma observes that 'Both the East and the West are rife with monsters of every stripe. Demons, dragons, ghosts, wrathful Buddhas, and supernatural animals occupy the theology, folklore, and daily rituals of religious cultures around the globe'.[57] In his pioneering essay on the history of monsters, 'Marvels of the East', Wittgower writes that 'Monsters — composite beings, half-human, half-animal — play a part in the thought and imagery of all peoples at all times. Everywhere the monster has been credited with the powers of a god or the diabolical forces of evil. Monsters have had their share in mythologies and fairy-tales, superstitions and prognostications'.[58] In *The Oxford Companion to World Mythology*, Leeming writes that 'All mythologies have monsters, nightmare creations that stand in the way of a hero's progress or that plague societies'.[59] Grotstein describes monsters as belonging to those numinous

56 Carey 2010.
57 Asma 2009, 14; cf. Lamb 1900.
58 Wittgower 1942, 197.
59 Leeming 2005, 268.

'*third forms* that have intimidated, enthralled, and ensorcelled mankind since the morning of time', and which continue 'to haunt the minds of human beings up through modern and unto present post-modern times'.[60] Many of these monsters, derived from forms of cultural poiesis and production, are something other than (or not quite, or no longer) human. They may even be embodiments of the *inhuman*. And yet I've also said that monsters can emerge from 'within' me.[61] For example, in addition to having dreams inhabited by monsters, I can see myself as a monster, or regard my thoughts or behaviour as monstrous, and other people can seem monstrous to me (and I to them). Thus in raising the problem of 'What are monsters?' we may also find that further, associated, questions emerge. What is it that makes something, or someone, 'monstrous'? Does being monstrous make one a monster? Or a monstrosity? Are thoughts about monsters also monstrous thoughts? Bailey argues that the 'human mind is laced with repressed emotions that we cast on to monsters; by creating monsters with undesirable human characteristics — such as envy, revenge, and selfishness — we are able to justify them within ourselves, which also makes us fear them'.[62]

But as this book seeks to demonstrate, monsters can also be 'good to think with'. For example, the philosopher Žižek, who has described himself as a monster, argues that each stage of capitalism throws up its own distinctive monsters (supposedly, we are currently in the epoch of the living dead, hence the proliferation of zombies).[63] Monsters readily give rise to metaphoric transpositions. In *Disparities* (2016), Žižek uses the figure of the Kraken (a sea monster from Nordic folklore) to describe the working of Hegel's philosophy: 'Hegel's thought effectively is a kind of philosophical giant squid, a dangerous and monstrous creature whose long conceptual tentacles enable it to exert an influence, often from invisible depths'.[64] Soon after, Žižek flips the metaphor, the Kraken standing in for global capitalism: 'Are our times [...] the times of capitalist modernity — not such an epoch of the awakened Kraken? Is Kraken not a perfect image of global Capital, all-powerful and stupid, cunning and

60 Grotstein 1997, 49.
61 Cf. Bailey 2008, 9.
62 Bailey 2008, 9.
63 Žižek 1991; see also McNally 2011; Sutcliffe 2011; Draus and Roddy 2016; Steven 2017; Jones 2018, 49–58.
64 Žižek 2016, 1.

blind, whose tentacles regulate our lives?'[65] Here we find two striking uses of a monster as a metaphor in contemporary critical theoretical discourse, in this case suggesting that the giant squid of Hegel's philosophy can aid us in making sense of the Kraken of global capitalism.

Embodied thinking about monsters stirs the play of imaginary significations into new motions and perhaps draws our attention to the mutability of forms (metamorphosis). These two forms of dynamism — of imaginary significations and of forms — are important to emphasise. I will suggest that in existential terms monsters emerge from the conjunction of the movement of imaginary significations and the mutability of forms encountered in human experience of terrestrial existence. This is not simply to say that monsters are an epiphenomenon of the psyche–world interaction, or mere figments of sensory-perceptual ambiguity. Rather, that (consciousness of, *and as*) metamorphosis — the transformation of forms — is a condition of possibility for the creation of monsters. Monsters dissolve stable forms and reorganise them into new configurations.

The very embodiment of monsters is usually a manifestation of these potencies. The dynamism of forms is thus a key element of the phenomenology of monsters. George Canguilhem, in his lecture on 'Monstrosity and the Monstrous',[66] drew attention to a relationship between the dynamic movement of the imagination and the monstrous. For Canguilhem, the 'power of the imagination is inexhaustible, indefatigable [...] Imagination [...] is nourished only by its own activity [...] it incessantly deforms or reforms the old images in order to make new ones. *In this way we see that the monstrous, inasmuch as it is imaginary, proliferates'.*[67] This relationship between the flux of imaginary significations and the proliferating figuration of monsters should be underlined: the implication is that the human psyche continually throws up new figurations of monsters.

---

65 Ibid., 3.
66 Delivered in Brussels, 1962.
67 Canguilhem 1962, 41; emphasis added.

Homo monstrosus and the Dragons of Eden (Or, 'Do Monsters Dream?')

Among the earliest forms of human self-awareness was the awareness of being meat.[68]

We could go so far as to say that it is the human condition to be grotesque, since the human animal is the one that does not fit in, the freak of nature who has no place in the natural order and is capable of re-combining nature's products into hideous new forms.[69]

The Hippocampus was a horse with fish-like tail, on which gods of the sea are often represented riding.[70]

Once we begin to look more closely, then, it seems that monsters proliferate throughout the plane of human existence (in its various dimensionalities). Accordingly, we can suggest that monsters are phenomena that are *essentially* grounded in the field of human existential experience. I do not mean to imply that monsters are thereby necessarily mere subjective phantasms lacking any substantive or corporeal 'reality'. No. Rather, that the interpretative (and pre-interpretive) processes through which something (or someone) is taken to be a monster derive in each and any case from the human (biocultural) constitution of existential meanings and values. In other words, *so far as we know*, it is only human beings that engage with the world in ways that involve *monster-making*. At the same time, we should acknowledge that in delimiting the sphere of monster-making to human beings we might also be manifesting an anthropocentric anxiety about the porousness of boundaries between different species (such anxieties are a common theme in the literature around monsters and human 'speciesism').[71]

And yet all of this, perhaps, is to assume some more or less intuitive notion of what a monster is, some already established capacity for recognising, naming, labelling, classifying, and/or otherwise identifying particular entities as monsters. Where might such a propensity come from? In this chapter I am

---

68 Quammen 2003, 3.

69 Fisher 2016, 35.

70 Harvey 1937, 279.

71 Cf. Thomas 1987; Midgley 2011; Tsing et al. 2017b; Ulstein 2017.

assuming that it is something *mostly* learned through human culture. More precisely, the forms that monsters take are strongly influenced by cultural horizons of meaning. From a critical anthropological perspective, however, it is also necessary to leave space for the role of phylogenetic factors that have impacted human evolution. Indeed, while culturalist perspectives are dominant in the flourishing field of academic monster studies, it is also possible to argue that human experiences of monsters are at least partly derived from biological and evolutionary sources that are more or less outside, beyond, or perhaps even prior to, the domain of human culture and the realm of learned experiences. On this view, monsters derive from ancient strands of our evolutionary heritage and have their ultimate provenance in the deep time of the history of life on earth. The 'monster within' may be seen as rooted in the ancient structures of the human brain.[72]

Hybrid (biocultural) positions somewhere between the cultural and biological poles of this spectrum are also not uncommon. For example, from a perspective that synthesizes Jungian archetypal theory and neuroscience, Stevens argues that monsters can be conceived as 'evolutionary, neurological, and psychological constructs'.[73] On this view, monsters are regarded as examples of the 'kind of symbols humans can create out of their own atavistic propensities encoded in the reptilian and palaeo-mammalian components of their brains'.[74]

Or...are these simply modern iterations of an ancient narrative form in which serpentine monsters (e.g., Tiamat, Leviathan) emerge from *chaos* or are coextensive with the great encircling ocean at the boundaries of the known world (and from which the world was sometimes imagined to have emerged)? We find monsters lurking in the depths of cosmogonic and anthropogonic speculation across a spectrum from ancient mythology to modern science. Here, they mingle and interbreed with the gods and help us make sense of the evolution of biological forms. Writing about 'monstrous births', Canguilhem contended that 'it is only because we men are living beings that a morphological failure is, *in our eyes*, a monster'.[75] More recently, in *Arts of Living on a Damaged Planet*, Tsing et al. write that 'Life has been monstrous almost from its beginnings. In ancient times, prokaryotes [...] gave birth to monsters in

---

72 E.g., Sagan 1978.

73 Stevens 1999, 368.

74 Ibid., 370.

75 Canguilhem 1962, 27; emphasis added.

which one organism engulfed others or joined immoderate liaisons, forming nucleated cells and multicellular organisms called eukaryotes. Ever since, we have muddled along in our mixes and messes. All eukaryotic life is monstrous'.[76]

If nature can create 'monsters' ('in our eyes'), it is humans who remain *the* monster-making animal. Are our monsters vestigial remnants of our ancestral past lived in the midst of other creatures? I can merely speculate here. I am not attempting a contribution to paleopsychology.[77] Certainly, we know that other zoological species can recognise threats (e.g., predators) in their environments, and some even communicate this information to their conspecifics, but we still do not know of other biological creatures that tell each other stories about monsters. We also understand the emotion of fear as deriving from organismic functions and patterns of neurological integration that are biologically ancient and widely distributed among vertebrate species, and that other mammals experience fear.[78] We are even fairly certain that some organisms experience something akin to human dreaming, but we do not have accounts of the contents of these 'dreams'.

Humans, however, begin dreaming about monsters at a very early age. Some research suggests that children dream about monsters and wild animals more frequently than adults (however, this may vary when adults live in environments with relatively higher coefficients of adversity).[79] Here I cite at some length an extremely suggestive passage from Coolidge and Wynn's *The Rise of Homo sapiens* (2009), in which they synthesise material on children's dream reports:

> Dream reports of modern children provide possible insights into the life and consciousness of early hominins. Van der Castle and Domhoff, in large surveys of children's dream reports, found that animal characters made up the largest proportion of children's dreams (approximately 20 percent to 45 percent). They noted that the animals in dreams tended to be those that were not often encountered in children's actual lives, e.g., monsters, bears, wolves, snakes, gorillas, tigers, lions, and biting insects, although children do often dream of commonly encountered animals such

76 Tsing, Swanson, Gan, and Bubant 2017a, M5.
77 Instead see Bailey 1986.
78 Cf. LeDoux 2012.
79 Coolidge and Wynn 2009, 137, 139.

as cats and dogs. The authors also noted that college students and older individuals, whose percentage of animal dreams was much lower, tended to dream of animals more likely to be encountered in real life, e.g., horses, dogs, and cats. Children's dreams also had higher rates of aggression than adult dreams, and higher rates of aggression involving animals. Revonsuo interprets these findings in terms of threat-simulation theory, which states that the present dream-production system simulates threatening events in the ancestral environment.[80]

For Coolidge and Wynn, this material is suggestive in relation to the interpretation of the evolution of hominin cognition, and applies to the possibility that our ancestors may have developed more elaborate dreaming scenarios as part of the 'tree-to-ground sleep transition', since 'life on the ground was inordinately more dangerous'.[81] In this hypothetical scenario, dreaming is understood as a biological function that includes threat-simulation and Coolidge and Wynn argue that it 'appears highly probable that threatening ancestral environments helped sustain threatening dream themes in early hominins'.[82] In ordinary language, this perspective suggests that modern humans have inherited a way of dreaming that has deep roots in prehistory and which may be related to the changing ecological contexts that our hominin ancestors inhabited. In short, as our ancestors

descended

from

the

trees,

the increasing vulnerability of hominin bodies to the threat of predators on the ground had the evolutionary consequence of eliciting more elaborate dreams about monsters.

The possible relationship between the human propensity for monster-making and the lived experience of the threat of predation is a recurrent theme in modern naturalistic accounts of the aetiology of monsters.[83] Stevens argues that 'Monsters are nightmare fossils living in our minds. They relate us directly

80 Ibid., 137–38.
81 Ibid., 129–30.
82 Ibid., 139.
83 E.g., Stevens 1999; Quammen 2003; Kaplan 2013.

to our primeval origins, and they come out at night to threaten us in our dreams. They are hideous manifestations of the archetype of the huge-jawed, slavering, heavily clawed predator, capable of seeking us out wherever we hide'.[84] In *Monster of God: The Man-Eating Predator in the Jungles of History and the Mind*, Quammen writes that 'Great and terrible flesh-eating beasts have always shared landscape with humans. They were part of the ecological matrix within which *Homo sapiens* evolved. They were part of the psychological context in which our sense of identity as a species arose. They were part of the spiritual systems that we invented for coping'.[85] He continues with the confronting suggestion that 'Every once in a while, a monstrous carnivore emerged like doom from a forest or a river to kill someone and feed on the body. It was a familiar sort of disaster [...] And it conveyed a certain message. *Among the earliest forms of human self-awareness was the awareness of being meat*'.[86] This line of thought, that the human psyche has been shaped by the evolutionary context of predator–prey dialectics, and that our oneiric experiences manifest traces of this prehistory, implies that humans are endogenously prone to monster-making. Putting a phrase from Carl Sagan to misuse, we can call this the 'Dragons of Eden' approach to the aetiology of monsters.[87]

But in addition to putative phylogenetic foundations, the aetiology of monsters also has a basis in ontogeny.[88] Here we are on less speculative terrain. We should distinguish here between a pan-human monster-making propensity and the diversity of lived contexts in which particular monsters take on their distinctive forms. In anthropological terms, we could suggest that the processes of socialisation in any human cultural life-world will potentially include an initiation into the world(s) of monsters. In this sense, in a point that is difficult to overemphasise, they are part of the human repertoire of socialising tools. Nevertheless, the anthropological question of whether, from the internal horizons of meaning in any particular cultural life-world, such entities are always known in terms that are analogous to 'our' conventional ideas about monsters must remain open.

Monsters may ostensibly be figured as emerging from the abyss of the unknown, and indeed they do, as threatening forms that terrify us, as indeed

84 Stevens 1999, 367.
85 Quammen 2003, 3.
86 Ibid. Emphasis added.
87 Sagan 1978.
88 Cf. Bailey 2008.

they are; but their widespread manifestations in human experience — in terms of both individual psychology and at the level of cross-cultural comparison — suggest that they are also our intimate familiars. That our first personal encounters with monsters usually take place at a very early age underscores this intimate familiarity.[89] Indeed, one might say that the process of becoming human involves learning about how to live with monsters.

Out of the One, Many: Unbridled Speculations on Monstrous Proliferations

> The analysis that focuses on the 'ideological meaning' of monsters overlooks the fact that, before signifying something, before serving as a vessel of meaning, monsters embody enjoyment qua the limit of interpretation, that is to say, *nonmeaning as such*.[90]

> The logic of monsters is one of particulars, not essences. Each monster exists in a class by itself. Monsters may, however, generate entire classes of beings.[91]

We have seen that monsters can be encountered as part of internal and external experience, that we learn about them in childhood, and that they may have roots deep in our evolutionary history as a species. *Arguably*, they are universal features of diverse human socio-cultural worlds. Although they are predominantly construed as threatening and often feared, we have also seen that people may find monsters 'good to think with'. I want to conclude with some broad statements about monsters that return to the theme of the ways they evade definitive interpretation.

Throughout my discussion I have repeated, perhaps to excess, that monsters are not stable forms. However, at the risk of belabouring the point, this instability can be understood in two further senses. First, to say that monsters are not stable forms can apply to a typical aspect of monsters, *viz*., that they are mixtures, or 'hybrid' forms. In the Preface to the first edition of *The Book of Imaginary Beings*, Borges tells us that 'a monster is no more

89 Cf. Sharon and Wooley 2004.
90 Žižek 1991, 54.
91 Weiss 2004, 124.

than a composition of parts of real beings'.[92] However, by suggesting that monsters are $^{uns}ta_{ble}$ forms, I have also pointed to the fact that monsters, and that which is taken to be monstrous, change over time. In other words, the very *conceptualization* of monstrosity and the monstrous is something that changes through time.[93] Hence the necessity of asking what *has been meant* by monsters. Or, what have monsters meant?

In addition to the problem of many monsters, the slipperiness of the category itself, the shifts in the meaning of 'monster', the hybridity of monsters, and the changeability of conceptions of monstrosity and the monstrous we find, too, that monsters themselves often have a metamorphic or shape-shifting dimension. Here we might think of werewolves (as transformative) or, alternatively, (the entity in) the classic sci-fi movie, *The Blob* (1958) — with its accompanying promotional tagline 'Terror has no shape' — as an exemplary instance of an amorphous monster. But metamorphoses and transformations are virtually ubiquitous aspects of the phenomenology of monsters.[94] Dell suggests that the ability of monsters to change their form is one of their 'more unnerving properties'.[95] This (morphodynamic) capacity to manifest in indeterminate and/or changing form is one way that monsters can resemble aspects of the phenomenology of human experiences of fear. Monsters can exceed limits and destroy boundaries, through the irruptive force of their manifestations, transforming order into chaos. They are archetypal 'disturbers of the peace'. In the process (often one of rampaging destruction), monsters can also disrupt rigid classificatory schemes and hierarchies, throwing conventional polarities such as mind/body, human/animal, alive/dead, natural/unnatural, tame/wild, self/other, same/different, inside/outside, imaginary/real, conception/perception, etc. into disorder. Milburn suggests that 'monsters disrupt totalizing conceptions of nature and destroy taxonomic logics, at once defining and challenging the limits of the natural'.[96] They are thus ambiguous and ambivalent, even polyvalent, figures. This means that monsters make 'ideal' figures for the signification of regions of human practice where old or established boundaries are being challenged by new ensembles and configurations.

92 Borges 2002, 14.
93 Cf. Goss 2012; Koudounaris 2016.
94 Cf. Dell 2016, 126–39.
95 Ibid., 126.
96 Milburn 2003, 604; cf. Midgley 2011, 155.

Philosopher Mary Midgley has also drawn attention to this aspect of monsters in the context of an analysis of changing conceptions of human–animal relationships and the problem of species boundaries:

> Traditional mixed monsters — minotaurs, chimeras, lamias, gorgons — stand for deep and threatening disorder, something not just confusing but dreadful and invasive. Although benign monsters such as Pegasus and archangels are occasionally found, in general the symbolism of mixing species is deeply uncanny and threatening. Even less mixed monsters, such as giants and three-headed dogs, are so framed as to violate the principles of construction that normally make life possible for their species. They too are usually seen as alien and destructive forces.[97]

I can concur, then, with Canguilhem's observation that 'The existence of monsters calls into question the capacity of life to teach us order'.[98] Like fears and anxieties, monsters often inhabit the shadowy borderlands between the known and the unknown (including: difference, otherness, exteriority, etc.). As 'denizens of the borderland',[99] they are thus liminal figures that mediate transitions between these domains and exchanges across their frontiers.

What is a monster?

What are monsters?

These are thorny questions to attempt to answer in a short exploratory piece. But in conclusion, let me consider some possibilities (each of these, I should emphasise, involves an interpretation that transforms monsters into something else).

Are monsters products of our imagination?

Or are they cultural symbols of collective fears and anxieties? Perhaps they are denizens of the boundary region between the known and the unknown; the familiar and the strange?

Maybe they are representations of threats to the symbolic order?

Or tropes from various shades of political rhetoric?

Or even mythical creatures from before the world was formed? Could monsters be neuropsychological vestiges of our evolutionary heritage?

Or constellations of negative qualities that are projected onto

97 Midgley 2011, 155.

98 Canguilhem 1962, 27.

99 Milburn 2003, 603.

demonised categories of people?

Or merely frightening yet seductive figures from folkloric narratives and the fairy-tales that are told to children?

Are monsters creatures that emerge from our dreams?

Or fabulous beasts known from medieval bestiaries and ancient travellers' tales?

Are monsters human or non-human (or both)?

Should we seek them in our cultural experience or our biological morphology?

Are they culturally-specific constellations of meaning, or pan-human symbolic archetypes (e.g., of primal fears)?

Maybe monsters are functional significations of genuine existential threats?

Or significations of the disordering of nature?

No doubt, other possible interpretations could be added to this brief list of suggestive possibilities. However, a different point can also be made about the interpretability of monsters and their multifarious forms. Considered in terms of the problem at hand — *what is it that monsters are taken to be?* — it turns out that monsters may be any and all of these things (and in fact are not limited to these possibilities alone). Indeed, as Halberstam argues in *Skin Shows: Gothic Horror and the Technology of Monsters*, 'excessive interpretability' is a hallmark of the monstrous,[100] and one that has enabled this very book — itself a work of bricolage. This excess, coupled with the chimerical multiplicity of potential forms that monsters may take, not to mention the frequently metamorphic dynamism of their manifestations, constitutes the broad problem region of polymorphous monstrosity.

Chimera — A Post Script

Hybrid, indecipherable, undetermined, hellish, interpretable, feminine, metaphorical, light, animal, fiery, raging, boundless, impossible, Chimera is the only monster which, when transformed from myth into language, brought along the same allurement, the same threat.[101]

Should a totem power animal be required for this essay into the realm of monsters, to assist in warding off the generalist risk of abstraction while helping to anchor the imagination in something more concrete, one monster

---

100 Halberstam 1995.
101 Bompiani 1989, 401.

in particular suggests herself. Insofar as our general discussion can be related to a singular example of a monster, it is perhaps the figure of the Chimera (or Chimaera; from the Greek Χίμαιρα, *Chímaira*: 'she-goat') that has the most intrinsic relation to what has been said here about what monsters are. This is in part because the Chimera is emblematic of metamorphic transformations of form, on the one hand, and also because of her hybrid embodiment (comprising elements of the lion, goat and snake), on the other. The Chimera is not just any hybrid, though; rather, as Bompiani emphasises, 'she is the supreme hybrid'.[102] The Chimera's hybridity is not solely one of composite embodiment but also includes her dual aspect of being both wild and tame. What is more, the historical career of the Chimera in the Occidental civilisational tradition — from Mediterranean and Near Eastern myths, through Greco-Roman mythography and Latin epic poetry, to Romano-Christian texts and then late medieval and Renaissance mythography, art, literature, and beyond — is closely representative of certain pathways of transmission, through which numerous monsters have come down to us from the worlds of ancient civilisations. Surprisingly, perhaps, the Chimera was virtually unknown to medieval art and does not feature in medieval bestiaries.[103] Bompiani notes that for Greek and Roman writers the Chimera is always depicted as either being killed or as being an impossibility. However, for Renaissance and also modern writers, the Chimera is usually approached in terms that focus on her meaning. This is related to a movement from the 'imaginary' to the 'symbolic' as the Chimera moves from myth into iconic and emblematic forms, as a complex signifier, before becoming a figure of speech, the 'metaphor of metaphor'[104]: 'the being that could not exist has become supremely interpretable', 'a composite but an unstable composite [...] a figure which tends to decompose and recompose in a thousand different ways'.[105] The Chimera is also notable for her transformation into the modern word 'chimera'. From the later sixteenth century, the semantic range of the English word 'chimera' began to expand away from the mythological creature, becoming a general term denoting 'A mere wild fancy; an unfounded conception'[106], and this signification of irreality has become the conventional sense in modern usage (for example: 'A chimerical

102 Bompiani 1989, 373.
103 Ibid., 383.
104 Ibid., 377, 387.
105 Ibid., 377, 387.
106 SOED, I: 325.

force has been rampaging through global markets in recent months, wreaking widespread havoc'). There is a certain movement of disenchantment in this becoming chimerical of the Chimera: the 'patchwork image disappeared but the word remained, signifying the impossible'.[107] But here we can also see that monsters sometimes disappear into our language.

107 Borges 2002, 42.

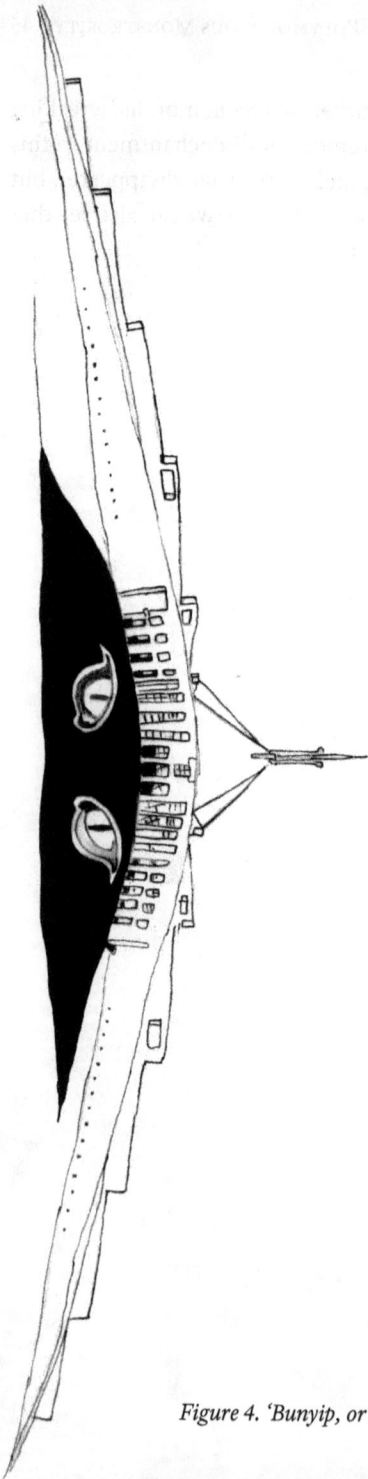

Figure 4. 'Bunyip, or Beneath Canberra', by Al Gevers.

IV
The Bunyip, and Other Australian Monsters

The bunyip wandered sadly along the creek. 'Will someone tell me what bunyips look like?' he said, to anyone who would listen. But there was no answer. Further along the creek he met a man. The man was busy with his notebook and pencil, and did not look at the bunyip. [...] The bunyip waited for a long time, and then he said very slowly and clearly, 'Can you please tell me what bunyips look like?' 'Yes, Bunyips don't look like anything [...] Bunyips simply don't exist.' [...] The bunyip was shaken. Then he sighed a long, deep sigh. [...] And he walked slowly back to his waterhole.[1]

SPEAKING IN LONDON IN OCTOBER 2017, THE FORMER AUSTRALIAN PRIME Minister Tony Abbott invoked the anachronistic trope of primitivism to argue against taking action on climate change. He said, 'primitive people once killed goats to appease the volcano gods, we are more sophisticated now but are still sacrificing our industries and our living standards to the climate gods to little more effect'. Mr Abbott is well known for his hostility to science and his professed Catholic faith (a belief system that includes belief in sacrifices of 'blood and flesh' to a paternal sky god). As the self-appointed spokesperson for a reactionary, denialist tendency in Australian public life, this quagmire of a statement is a good place to begin a discussion about monsters in Australia, where this book is written. This act of thinking about monsters in Australia

1 *The Bunyip of Berkeley's Creek* by Jenny Wagner, 1973.

involves directly facing the postcolonial dilemmas of a settler-colonial society deeply unresolved about its relationship to Indigenous peoples, its history of violent dispossession, and the land itself. To think about monsters in the context of the global Anthropocene — the new epoch of catastrophic human-induced changes to the earth and its systems, which is already well advanced in Australia, as elsewhere — is to take our efforts in this book from being a seemingly playful cultural history, to ontological concerns about our capacity to respond to this crisis.

This chapter was written by Peter in the State Library of Victoria, an institution built on the promise of the Enlightenment ideals of universal knowledge and scientific reason. This European urban order has been superimposed over *Naarm*, the Indigenous Woiwurrung name for this part of Kulin peoples' country otherwise known as Melbourne. Situated on the crest of a small hill which rolls down to the River Birrarung (Yarra) at a key intersection on Melbourne's nineteenth-century geometric grid of north–south, east–west streets, the library is a prominent neo-classical urban landmark next to the technical university where we, the authors, all work. Inside, I sit under the capacious dome of the Reading Room as sunlight shines down on hundreds of studious Melbournians working diligently at their desks. The sunlight also illuminates four vast levels of book stacks, designed to inspire a sense of awe for the powerful knowledge systems of the pre-digital British Empire. It is not an exaggeration to say that this is a place, despite being founded on secular values, that carries a sense of sanctity; it is a potent node for reflection within the global network of white systems of knowledge-power. All around me the young (whose lives will see the greatest impacts of climate change) work on school or university assignments; we older denizens work on historical research, a novel, or apocrypha such as this reflection on monsters, while outside the weather is unseasonal, yet again.

Through this period of writing and reflection I have also been working with — and being educated and influenced by — Gunnai and other Aboriginal people around Lake Tyers in East Gippsland. Lake Tyers is only four hours' drive from the State Library (no great distance by Australian standards), but it is a world away in terms of thinking about 'country'. In Aboriginal English country carries a deep sense of ancestral connection to place, of places as being alive in themselves, and of place and people relating deeply to one another. Country can be nurturing and kind, but is not only benign; places can also be troubled by bad events (like massacres), memories, spirits of the dead, and spirit beings. I described the State Library as sitting on the city grid, but also dwelling in Kulin peoples' country. This monument to rationality sitting on living country is an ideal place to start thinking about 'irrational' phenomena such as monsters, and specifically Australian monsters like bunyips.

This chapter suspends the standard Enlightenment binaries of mythical and real, irrational and rational, here and there, local and universal, in order to listen more carefully to this country, its people, and its monsters. This suspension opens a space for monsters and their country to speak back critically to the universality of the Enlightenment. Like other chapters in this volume, it embraces monsters and monstrosity for what they have to teach us about ourselves, to open up our perceptions of the present and change our futures. Taking these monsters seriously helps us navigate the intellectual swamplands of radical relativity. Acknowledging our specifically Australian monsters, we also find ourselves enmeshed in a specific, local version of the (supposedly universal) Enlightenment, rather than a fully postmodern relativism that rejects all Enlightenment claims. This chapter takes inspiration from both anthropological moves to examine universal claims through the lens of an alter-ontology and direct critiques of the colonising logic of 'Postcolonial Reason'.[2]

The Library also hosts icons of irrationality, myth, and legend. Thrown together somewhat randomly over time, the scale of accumulation of these statues creates the effect of an underlying institutional counter-narrative. If you were to walk with me through the library forecourt, we would see that a series of apparently unrelated statues and sculptures do this referential work, linking the mythical, the monstrous, and the model citizen. The most prominent statues guarding either side of the library entrance are a mounted Joan of Arc in full armour, and a muscular mounted Saint George, driving his spear into a writhing dragon. Between them, at the heart of the magnificent domed Reading Room (modelled after the British Museum's) is a statue of the room's namesake, Justice Sir Redmond Barry. This colonial era judge was credited with founding the Library and other definitive civic institutions including the Royal Melbourne Hospital, and was the first Chancellor of the University of Melbourne. Barry is best remembered as the presiding judge who sentenced to death Australia's legendary folk hero, and outlaw bushranger Ned Kelly. In another irony, Kelly's iconic steel body armour is housed (like a holy relic) in a permanent exhibition inside the library Barry founded.

2 Spivak 1999; Mignolo 2011.

If we then look to one side of the forecourt steps, we see a discrete metre-high bronze of an Indigenous Australian monster, the bunyip (the portrayal of which is based on the illustrated book that opens this chapter), and a sculpture of the 'gumnut babies'. Both of these sculptures are based on illustrations from much-loved twentieth-century Australian children's literature, and both are attempts towards a local, environmentally grounded (and white) Australian mythology. They are efforts to have something enchanting to tell the children born in a country founded on disenchantment and stubborn silence about the foundational acts of land theft, mass murder, cultural erasure, and denial of any resistance by Aboriginal people.

But there was resistance. One famous instance involves Tasmanian warriors Tunnerminnerwait and Maulboyheenner running a war of resistance in Gippsland. After their defeat in 1841 they were put on trial for murder and found themselves defended by our library founder Redmond Barry in an earlier role as public legal defender of Aborigines standing trial. To his credit Barry questioned the authority of the court to try these men under British law and argued the evidence against them was dubious and circumstantial. Despite this defence the result was a forgone conclusion, the accused were not allowed to give evidence, were found guilty, and hanged in a public execution in 1842 within sight of the Library, on what is now our RMIT University campus.

Not far from the bunyip statue we can see a life-size likeness of Superintendent of the Port Phillip District at that time (later Governor) La Trobe; he was another key agent of colonial order and the violence it brought with it. These two foundational figures (La Trobe and the bunyip) have a necessary historical relationship, for bunyips were very much on La Trobe's mind. Historian Kristen Otto writes that Charles La Trobe,

> wrote in 1847 of the constant rumours of 'some unknown beast'. He was convinced of their existence and various Kulin provided sketches for him of this very large billabong-and-river based creature, somewhat resembling a plesiosaurus. La Trobe stated, 'It is pretended that before the Europeans arrived the Yarra near Melbourne possessed many of them'.[3]

These sculptural supplements at the State Library inadvertently pay homage to the very things that the universal march of scientific reason promised to

3   Otto 2005, 149.

dispel: legendary heroes, saints, outlaws, mystics, and monsters — they are all included here alongside the Governor and the Judge in the great orbit of the Library. Characteristically celebrated by artistic and literary Romanticism, these iconic figures provide an emotional, even mystical foundation for rational Enlightenment values: the Freudian Id to the institutional Superego. The Enlightenment project was to dispel the darkness of superstition and irrationality with the light of science and reason; no more 'sacrificing goats to volcano gods'. This *should* also mean squarely facing the facts of Australian colonial history, upholding the principles of universal human rights, offering young people a viable, hopeful future, and acknowledging the science of global warming, yet on all these fronts Australian political culture is failing, and spectacularly so.

As Spivak, Mignolo, Moreton-Robinson,[4] and many others argue, the Enlightenment project is deeply entwined with the facts of colonising power, which undermine and contradict its core tenets. The classic example is the revolutionary French Republic declaring all men free and equal in brotherhood, yet refusing to extend this universal truth to slaves and women whose subjection underwrote the dominant forms of production and accumulation. The next two hundred years were spent in the epic struggle over this contradiction we call modern history, and despite Francis Fukuyama's late-twentieth century triumphalism contained in his much-derided book *The End of History*, it's far from resolved. In Australian political culture the symptoms of Enlightenment reason's subordination to settler-colonial power has reached a moment that could be described in popular cultural terms as 'peak whiteness,' a moment when the absurdities and contradictions are on full display. Library founder Redmond Barry, whose aforementioned statue stands among these monsters, would be perplexed at such an intellectual stalemate in his glorious civic outpost of the imperium. Universal reason was to triumph over darkness in all its forms: Irish Roman Catholic outlaws, native superstitions, ignorance, and the base self-interest of coal barons and newspaper tycoons. Yet here we are.

In these increasingly desperate and exasperating circumstances, which perplex so many Australians' attempts to be 'good citizens' within this Enlightenment tradition, we need to find moments in which we can break out of the grid of modernity and look at this country very differently. In 1972, the year before my father first read me the children's book about the sad, colonised bunyip in *The Bunyip of Berkeley's Creek*, the city was stopped by a deluge. The

4   Spivak 1999; Mignolo 2011; Moreton-Robinson 2015.

great flood of my childhood saw rain thunder down on the city grid with a burst of such intensity that roads became waterways. Torrents poured off the library dome, and just down the hill a flooding creek came pouring over the top of where Elizabeth Street had been minutes earlier. My father was trapped in the Argus newspaper building as this creek roared by, carrying cars and benches and rubbish bins in its rush to meet the Yarra River, the intersection being a Wurundjeri sacred site. What I understand from this flood is that there was always a living waterway under Elizabeth Street, that our city grid had been stubbornly imposed over another order, and for a moment the old places had returned to living memory and could do so again. The monsters in the library forecourt offer that same possibility for realisation if we shift from seeing them as romantic supplements, and instead take them rather more seriously as beings embedded in our lives. Among these monsters at the library, the swamp-dwelling bunyip will now be our guide through this intellectual and political quagmire, and lead us towards an Australian intellectual project beyond colonising binaries.

The Bunyip

The bunyip is the most widely recognised monster assigned to the realm of mythology and folklore in the south-eastern part of Australia. Along the east coast of Australia it is more likely to be the hairy humanoid Yowie or Yahoo, first noted in the wake of Cook's voyage as 'The Great Hairy Wild Man of Botany Bay'.[5] Descriptions of the Australian bunyip vary widely. In summary, they are large, dangerous nocturnal creatures that inhabit swamps and waterways, are fast moving, short sighted, have large teeth, sometimes a long sharp beak or long snout, they have a restless appetite for human flesh and make terrifying noises. In the early colonial era bunyips became a significant object of intercultural concern, shuttling between Indigenous cultures and the settler-colonial imaginary at a critical time in the process of colonisers taking possession of the land and enforcing Aboriginal dispossession.

There are numerous early colonial reports of settlers sighting bunyips.[6] Newly arrived colonisers considered the possibility that this was, like the 'duck-billed platypus', another very elusive Australian zoological oddity awaiting discovery. The application of scientific knowledge to 'discovering,'

5   Jansen 2014.
6   Holden, 2001.

documenting, and mapping the country, its people, and animals was a practical undertaking, but also a key legitimating process linking the colonial project with European fantasies of an expanding 'civilisation'. The discovery of a giant skeleton of an extinct macropod at lake Bathurst in 1818 had brought the mythological creatures of the Eora and Gadigal peoples around Sydney face to face with Western scientific enquiry. The first written reference to this creature as a 'bunyip' appears in the *Geelong Advertiser and Squatters' Advocate*, in an 1845 report of fossils being found and identified as belonging to a bunyip. The article is worth quoting in full,

WONDERFUL DISCOVERY OF A NEW ANIMAL—In our last number we gave an account of the finding of a fragment of the knee joint of some gigantic animal, which, from there being no such animal hitherto known to exist in Australia, we supposed to be the fossil remains of some early period. Subsequent information, however, coupled with the fact that the bone was in good preparation, and had altogether a 'recent' appearance, has induced us to alter our opinion.

On the bone being shown to an intelligent black, he at once recognized it as belonging to the 'Bunyip' which he declared he had seen. On being requested to make a drawing of it, he did so without hesitation.

The bone and the picture were then shown separately to different blacks who had no opportunity of communicating with each other; and they one and all recognised the bone and picture as belonging to the 'Bunyip,' repeating the name without variation.

One declared he knew where the whole of the bones of one animal were to be found; another stated his mother was killed by one of them, at the Barwon Lakes, within a few miles of Geelong, and that another woman was killed on the very spot where the punt crosses the Barwon at South Geelong. The most direct evidence of all was that of Mumbowran, who showed several deep wounds on his breast made by the claws of the animal. Another statement was made, that a mare, the property of Mr Furlong, was, about six years ago, seized by one of these animals on the bank of the Little River, and only escaped with a broken leg. They say that the reason why no white man has ever yet seen it, is because it is amphibious, and does not come on land except on extremely hot days when it basks on the bank; but on the slightest noise or whisper they roll gently over into the water, scarcely creating a ripple. We have adduced these authorities before giving a description of the animal, lest, from its strange, grotesque, and nondescript character, the reader should have at once set the whole down as fiction. The Bunyip, then, is represented as uniting the characteristics of a bird and of an alligator. It has a head resembling an emu with a long bill at the extremity of which is a transverse projection on each side, with serrated edges like the bone of the stingray. Its body and legs partake of the nature of the alligator. The hind legs are remarkably thick and strong, and the fore legs are much longer, but still of great strength. The extremities are furnished with long claws, but the blacks say its usual method of killing its prey is by hugging it to death. When in the water it swims like a frog, and when on shore it walks on its hind legs with its head erect, in which position it measures twelve or thirteen feet in height. Its breast is said to be covered with different coloured feathers: but the probability is that the blacks have not had a sufficiently near view to ascertain whether its appearance might not arise from hair or scales. They describe it as laying eggs of double the size of the emu's egg, of pale blue colour; these eggs they frequently meet with, but as they are 'no good for eating,' the black boys set them up for a mark, and throw stones at them.

We intend in a few days, to give a lithographic facsimile of the drawing made by the Black, so that our bush readers may be enabled to question the blacks in their own neighbourhood, and should any new facts be elicited, we shall take it as a favour in any one who may transmit an account of them to us for publication.[7]

The name bunyip has been sourced as coming from a number of related Kulin languages including the languages of the Wemba Wemba, the Wathaurrong (in the autobiography of William Buckley and the account above), and from the Boonwurrung peoples as 'bunyeep'. The first sketch of a bunyip was taken from the 'Challicum bunyip', a sacred earth carving of the bunyips' outline

---

7   *Geelong Advertiser and Squatters' Advocate* 1845.

maintained through annual ceremony by the Djabwurrung people from Western Victoria at Fiery Creek near Ararat. This sketch was taken in the 1840s, towards the end of the killing times — the genocidal war of conquest that raged over the incredibly lush, Indigenous-managed grasslands and waterways in the Western District of colonial Port Philip (now the state of Victoria) which brought the early colony such wealth when appropriated by the invaders as grazing lands for sheep.

As I drive east from Melbourne to meet with people in the Lake Tyers area, I first drive through areas rich in bunyip references. There is the town whose name is Bunyip, and it sits on the edge of what was once the vast and impenetrable Koo Wee Rup swamp. It was named by Boonwurrung people for its association with the swamp-dwelling creature. Those swamps have now mostly been drained to make rich farmland for dairy grazing and growing spears of asparagus, and only a small area set aside as protected wetland, feeding crucial nutrients into the waters of Westernport Bay so famous for the leafy sea dragons Julian mentioned in our book's beginning. Bunyips and dragons are connected by more than the State Library forecourt, they are ecologically connected as swamp is to mangroves and bay sea grasses — the dangerous bunyip protects the shy sea dragon!

Empty Land

In much the same way as the Enlightenment project split and sequestered its darker impulses into Romanticism, Australia has functioned as a space of irrational excess in the European imaginary over centuries. The idea of an unknown great southern land, Terra Australis Incognita, provided the European Renaissance imagination from the sixteenth century until the Age of Discovery, with a 'great southern land' inhabited by all manner of monsters and used as a literary and artistic fictional setting of endless possibility. Once 'discovered' and documented by the late eighteenth-century English and French scientific expeditions, Australian flora, fauna, and native peoples provided European science with another space for imagining radical difference. In the natural world the discovery of the kangaroo, black swan, and platypus provided evidence of this radical alterity. In the domain of European thinking about human evolution and cultural difference, these expeditions provided the basis for descriptions of 'primitive man' (or in the French case 'noble savage'), upon which European claims of civilisational superiority relied. Spivak provides a thorough critical account of how these projections figure in the 'anthropological' work of Kant, Hegel, and Marx.[8] In the early twentieth century this increasingly detailed Australian anthropological record became intimately entwined with the currents of European modernity through works such as Durkheim's *Elementary Forms of the Religious Life*,[9] and Freud's *Totem and Taboo*.[10]

Colonial encounters in Australia show a concern with establishing a scientific understanding of nature as an act of possession[11] while simultaneously struggling to make sense of this country through the inherited Eurocentric lens. The startling discoveries of black swans, marsupials, the remarkable platypus, and other strange creatures had inflamed the Enlightenment scientific imagination from the first accounts of the voyages of James Cook, Matthew Flinders, Nicolas Baudin, and others. As the early Sydney settlement began to push inland and explore the Australian interior this European knowledge entered very unfamiliar terrain: rivers that ran backwards to evaporate in the interior, seasons that varied between hyper-abundance and extreme scarcity, and supposedly primitive peoples who thrived and maintained a rich ceremonial and cultural life in this world of extreme variation. Enlightenment explorers, administrators, and scientists struggled to record these phenomena with the scientific objectivity they proclaimed, not least because the extension of this science was so utterly bound up with the project of territorial conquest and claims of civilisational superiority. Bruce Pascoe[12] and Bill Gammage[13] point to this contradiction in the early colonial accounts of Indigenous land use and settlements in the interior. They both point out that the observed facts of Aboriginal abundance in food production and storage for surplus, large permanent settlements, and rich cultural life were inconvenient, if not a direct contradiction, to the settler-colonial project of conquest over the 'empty' landscape of *terra nullius* (which Ani will revisit in the chapter that follows).

As the first people of the land were murdered, starved, and their cultures systematically and deliberately repressed, the bunyip and the spirits were driven further and further from connection with daily life on country, now dominated by colonising strangers. As Aboriginal people were dominated

8   Spivak 1999.
9   Durkheim 1912.
10   Freud 1913.
11   Moreton-Robinson 2015.
12   Pascoe 2015.
13   Gammage 2011.

by colonial violence, so was the bunyip. Eventually, bunyips became a disempowered artefact of 'Australiana' embedded in colonial culture, their true potency belittled and repressed by domestication, but still latent in country.

Settler-Colonial Monstrosity

As I drive on, passing from Boonwurrung country into Gunnai country, I have to face other kinds of monsters. After passing through what remains of the bunyip's domain, the important Koo Wee Rup swamp, the journey east takes me into the La Trobe Valley (yes, the Colonial Governor from the State Library yet again). This valley is notable for the massive billowing smoke stacks of the vast coal-fired power stations located here. These twentieth-century monoliths are some of the most carbon-intensive in the world, continuously burning the highly polluting brown coal found in the valley to power the city of Melbourne, keeping the lights on back at the State Library where we began this journey. Not only do these massive polluters fuel global warming, their presence in an area which has one of the highest rates of lung cancer in Australia, among other ills, is increasingly seen as uncoincidental. I drive past the town of Warragal (Gunnai for wild dog) and on towards Warrigal Creek in Gippsland, a vast region named arbitrarily after Governor La Trobe's successor Gipps. The indifference to places' proper Indigenous names in the colonising practice of foundational naming is a key performative act in taking possession of country, much like laying down a grid of roads over Naarm (inner Melbourne). Colonial science had the capacity to make systematic enquiries into these long-existing Indigenous place and species names, and to document them properly. The refusal to do so (with a few notable exceptions) up to this day, repeats the myth of *terra nullius* in a lazy and immature refusal of the clear evidence that these places have been fully inhabited and properly named for tens of thousands of years.

In July 1843, just two years prior to the jaunty colonial newspaper account of the bunyip story quoted earlier, a terrible massacre took place at Warrigal Creek. This was just one of many Gippsland massacres of Aboriginal family groups led by Scotsman Angus McMillan and his 'Highland Brigade'. That cold day they murdered between eighty and two hundred men, women, and children of the Bratowooloong clan camped by the creek. The list of massacre sites through Gippsland is chilling, not only for the genocidal horror they represent, but also for the gruesome names the massacres gave to these occupied places in the wake of dispossession: Boney Point, Butchers Creek, Skull Creek.

1840 — Nuntin — unknown number killed by Angus McMillan's men

1840 — Boney Point — 'Angus McMillan and his men took a heavy toll of Aboriginal lives'

1841 — Butchers Creek — 30–35 shot by Angus McMillan's men

1841 — Maffra — unknown number shot by Angus McMillan's me

1842 — Skull Creek — unknown number killed

1842 — Bruthen Creek — 'hundreds killed'

1843 — Warrigal Creek — between 60 and 180 shot by Angus McMillan and his men

1844 — Maffra — unknown number killed

1846 — South Gippsland — 14 killed

1846 — Snowy River — 8 killed by Captain Dana and the Aboriginal Police

1846–47 — Central Gippsland — 50 or more shot by armed party hunting for a white woman supposedly held by Aborigines; no such woman was ever found.

1850 — East Gippsland — 15–20 killed

1850 — Murrindal — 16 poisoned

1850 — Brodribb River — 15–20 killed[14]

As I drive on I have to pass by physical evidence of how Angus McMillan has been celebrated as the founding pioneer of the district and a fine upright citizen. Memorials, cairns, and place names (such as the federal electorate of McMillan, which was finally renamed in 2018 after protests from voters) all celebrate the man-monster who killed so many people for the sole purpose of taking possession of their land, undisturbed by their presence on it. Historical research has clearly identified him as 'the butcher of Gippsland,' something long known to Gunnai people who have to live in a community full of tributes to the killer of their ancestors (Elder, Gardner, Watson, Flyn). This is perversely similar to the celebration of the man-monster Ratko Mladić described by Hariz in such dreadful detail in this volume. Thanks to Hariz who introduced me to Bosnia, I twice looked Mladić directly in the eye while he stood trial in

14 See Gardener 2001.

The Hague in 2013 and 2014, and the chilling gaze of a psychopath shows not a chink of self-doubt or self-reflection, only bombastic self-justification. I can only imagine Angus McMillan had much the same kind of pathology.

Tragically, whole communities can hold these psychopathic (monstrous) killers up as exemplary heroes, denying the crimes they have committed and the lives and worlds they have destroyed. When the facts of genocide are denied, its guilty burden is split off from the cultural image of the good self, to be projected into myths blaming the monstrous non-humanness of the victims. In Australia this splitting permeates the dominant cultural imaginary: from the continuing Darwinian myth that Aboriginal people were responsible for their own destruction, through to the colonisation of the Indigenous bunyip. Today, finally, questions are being asked in the mainstream public sphere of settler-colonial Victoria (and some other parts of Australia) about the appropriateness of celebrating a figure such as McMillan; a surreptitiously state-sanctioned mass-murderer. If the project of any kind of truth and reconciliation between Indigenous and settler-colonial peoples is able to begin, we have to start with the evidence of crimes immediately in front of us, the names and the icons that are all around us.

Another step in this process is that we non-Indigenous peoples need to understand who we are in this land, starting with our collective name. In south-eastern Australia non-Indigenous people are commonly known to Indigenous people as 'Gubbahs'. The predominant assumption about the term Gubbah is that it is a bastardization of 'governor,' the colonial honorific form of address for ruling class men, or for 'government man' (convict). Peter Read contends, however, that the term is actually derived from the Northern Beaches area of Sydney's Gai-maragal language, giving it a monstrous provenance like so many other contact terms for European invaders throughout Australia and the Pacific. He writes,

The dangerous, hairy little people known as Gubjas — a word long in use, Denis [Foley] explains, before the Whites wrongly concluded that the word which Aboriginals use for them was derived from 'Gubna'. Gubjas on the other hand, were evil, ever on the watch for solitary Gai-maragal to kill the men, rape the women, rip open the stomach and eat the eyes. Part of their weaponry was their excrement-like stink [...] Watching from the foreshores, the Gai-mariagal judged that the sailors climbing the rigging of the

ships of the First Fleet were the Gubjas themselves, long known for
their agility in the trees, now daringly visible in broad daylight.[15]

Being a Gubbah in this country is not an entirely edifying thing by either
definition: monstrous or governmental! But recognising ourselves as Gubbahs,
and thus being in a more sympathetic communion with other monstrous
entities like bunyips, is a tentative step towards a decolonial presence on
country. Recognising ourselves on that side of the colonial–monstrous divide,
we might be better placed to recognise Indigenous peoples and powers not
as monstrous or deficient, but properly human. Unfortunately our dominant
cultural imaginary still largely sees our presence in Australia through a
European lens. Australia is still imagined as a place of monstrous natural
phenomena: huge man-eating sharks, crocodiles, poisonous snakes and
spiders, and the unpredictable violence of bush fire, cyclone, oppressive heat
waves, and flood. For the imaginary of European and North American media-
spheres, these antipodean excesses of nature are the main flow of newsworthy
material from Australia. The equation is a simple, mutually reinforcing binary
in the transcultural image economy: Australia is all (too much) nature, Europe
is all (too much) culture. This nature–culture binary is more than a mere trope
of Western thought, it is at the heart of the Western Enlightenment project,
from the philosophy of Descartes to the 'technophilia' of Silicon Valley's
engineered solutions to all our cultural and environmental woes. And it is a
broken paradigm.

Evidence of the exhaustion of this project is everywhere, but most
overwhelmingly in the fact of anthropogenic global warming, and the
creeping global awareness of the consequent catastrophic climate change that
has only just begun to be felt as 'strange weather'. Philosophy and culture are
increasingly struggling to catch up with the dawn of the anthropocene, which
decisively ends the old nature–culture binary.[16] Western thought now has to
account for the fact that we humans, and our systems of political economy,
culture, and production, are a decisive part of nature, and always were. Again,
Australian nature seems to be at the forefront of the consequences. In 2017 the
currents of climate denialism were theatrically staged as a pantomime play.
That year conservative government ministers gleefully passed around a lump
of coal in Parliament declaring, 'On this side of the house you will not find a fear

15 Read 2000, 218.
16 Bonneuil and Fressoz 2017.

of coal,'[17] echoing the previous Prime Ministers' declaration that, 'Coal is good for humanity'.[18] Six weeks after these coal-venerating theatrics, a catastrophic cyclone smashed the tropical Australian coastline and caused catastrophic damage to the already stressed Great Barrier Reef. Marine biologists reported the Great Barrier Reef was already suffering its largest ever warming-related 'coral bleaching event' when it was then hit by the cyclone, resulting in the mass death of over half the coral reef during 2016–17.[19] Around the same time a proposal for one of the worlds' largest coal mines was supported with the promise of Government financial incentives.[20] Despite these mounting catastrophes, triumphal capitalist nihilism and colonial denialism still hold a death grip on Australian political culture.

As will be explored later in this book, one cultural response to the destructive exploitation of the natural world by full-blown industrial capitalism has been the projection of this destructive force into the form of a monster. Similar arguments are made about the psychological motivation behind some of the more outlandish conspiracy theories, such as world events being orchestrated by alien lizard beings disguised as humans, a conspiracy of Jewish bankers or international freemasonry. This has led to a general tendency to dismiss these monster-theories from the mainstream of social or political critique to marginalia associated with the dark underside of modernity, whether romanticism or atavistic paranoia. Our proposition here is somewhat different. Consistent with a turn in anthropology to take ontological difference seriously as the possibility of multiple realities,[21] and in critical political theory to consider the interconnectedness of previously discrete phenomena,[22] this chapter sees the possibility to learn from and with our particular monsters — to take monsters seriously. Tamsin Kerr raises this question in regard to Australian planning regimes, arguing for planning 'as if bunyips mattered' as a radical step forward in an approach to landscape that reconciles with Indigenous understandings, and re-enchants Australian relationships with place.[23] Kerr gives the example of previous perceptions of

17 Haggarty 2017.
18 McKinnell 2014.
19 GBRMPA 2017.
20 Krien 2017.
21 Viveiros de Castro 2014.
22 Connolly 2013.
23 Kerr 2004.

'swampland' (the bunyip's home) as undesirable and unproductive, now being understood as environmentally crucial 'conservation wetlands'.

The next stage of a decolonial practice of 'bunyip thinking' is to take on the cultural and political implications of bunyips really mattering. In the midst of our myriad crises, engaging more seriously with our monsters offers some epistemological assistance to rethinking these tired paradigms. The bunyip is the most important of these properly mythical monsters to move from Indigenous cultures and country to find a way into the settler-colonial imaginary. We need to acknowledge and remember *our* potent monsters, bunyips and Gubbahs, now more than ever. Telling us where and who we really are, they may be the only things that can help us navigate our current, deep malaise.

V

Leviathan, the Sovereign

Going to the Shoreline

I WAS CERTAIN THAT THE STATE HAD AN APPETITE, FOR VIOLENCE. As a child Ani was taught about nationalism, and that nationalisms existed to oppress, to steal, and to justify murder. I was told that people often take up the legal apparatus, the symbols, and the language of the state with a terrifying intent. So, I should *beware* of it. My perception of 'the state' was also influenced by a literary diet of Western European and North American authors who had been shaped by the 'great wars'.[1] These classic texts philosophised about and grappled with the depredations and follies of nationalism, alongside the potentials of re-envisioned states and alternative political orders. They provided a certain world view, an internationalism peppered with anarchist idealism, exalting in individualism, often lamenting it, enamoured by the technical achievements of modernism, and *horrified* by them as well. Ideology, hope, desperation, and irony seeped from pages which were often shot through with a dark humour.[2]

A palpable and long shadow of tragedy seemed to fall across this century of literature. It felt to my younger self like there was, present in these texts, a kind of desperate engagement by the authors with a terrible reality that couldn't ever be avoided, by any of us. A courageous engagement with an ever-present doom, often framed in terms of statehood. What these books seemed to

1 Authors such as George Orwell, Aldous Huxley, George Bernard Shaw, Isaac Asimov, Ray Bradbury, Earnest Hemingway, and others.

2 E.g., Joseph Heller's (1961) novel *Catch 22*.

convey to me most strikingly about the experience of war was how it sunders the assumptions upon which we build lives with others. This world, between the covers of books, necessitated the kinds of questions that I was later to find Hannah Arendt engaging with in *The Origins of Totalitarianism*.[3] This world was a grim one, featuring the human capacity for cruelty and destruction, and its dance with political power and territory, and the banality of administrative processes. Omnipresent were questions of sovereignty, and of 'human nature'. Ever-present was the nation state.

But I grew up in a place with other kinds of nationalism than those present in these texts. Other kinds of territory and imagined communities,[4] sovereignties and citizenships, produced through colonialism and empire. Where a *common law* of empire (hypocritically) claimed to erase all that had come before, and yet was still anchored in a claim to stolen land.[5] These depictions of territory and sovereignty are more complex than the bounded nation state. But the various narratives I had inherited, to help me think about the problems of nationalism and the horror of the state, such as liberal egalitarianism, anarchist idealism, internationalist socialism, struggle to deal adequately with these realities of invasion and colonialism.

The quintessential turn-of-the-century British working-class novel (a favourite of my grandfather's) *The Ragged-Trousered Philanthropists* by Robert Tressell[6] provides one inroad into thinking through this. The overarching thread in the book is that workers who acquiesce to the exploitative status quo are acting in effect as *philanthropists*, giving away their labour, without just reward. However, while set-in working-class England the ideas engage more broadly with empire.

Tressell, drawing on his own experiences with imperialism, both as an Irish nationalist, and then as a 'poor white' in South Africa, tries hard in the text to draw out the irony of working for, but not benefiting from, empire. And the book contains moments of striking anti-imperialism. Indeed, according to Irish scholar Deaglán Ó Donghaile, 'As an immigrant himself, Noonan [Tressell's real name] was deeply aware of xenophobia as a technique used

---

3   Arendt 1973.

4   Anderson 2006.

5   Fitzpatrick 2002.

6   Tressell 1914/2018. Note: Tressell was a pen name; his real name Noonan. Contemporarily referred to as either.

by various powers to control public discourse'.[7] Yet, in reading we see that the hope of an emancipatory class-based politics, even an internationalist one, when coupled with a belief in the march of progress, can reveal an important irony.

One protagonist, who is struggling to convince his fellow workers of the importance of class struggle, extols the rights of all humans to the spoils of civilisation. But in so doing he subscribes to a narrative of modernity that relegates all that *came before* or is *other than* to a primitive past without value.[8] Imperial poverty is positioned in the text as 'particularly ironic given that the British working class were invited, via the South African War and imperialism, to enjoy some of the "benefits of civilization"'.[9] One analysis of this text claims that this reveals a disconcerting irony, which is that Tressell's '"imperialists in broken boots" may not be imperialists like Rhodes,[10] but they are [still] imperialists'.[11] In this way an internationalist politics, while rejecting the capitalist state, and the class politics of empire, can also align with empire and its depredations.

7   Ó Donghaile 2018, 381–83.

8   In one passage the language is especially egregious, and reveals this narrative, before outlining the book's egalitarian ethic: 'If a man is only able to provide himself and his family with the bare necessaries of existence, that man is living in poverty. Since he cannot enjoy the advantages of civilisation *he might just as well be a savage* [*sic*] [...] What we call civilisation — the accumulation of knowledge which has come down to us from our forefathers — is the fruit of thousands of years of human thought and toil. It is not the result of the labour of the ancestors of any separate class of people who exist today, and therefore it is by right the common heritage of all', p. 15 (my emphasis) Note: extensive comment/critique is available about the complex workings of empire, class, and colonialism in this text. See especially Cairnie 2002; Harker 2003; Ó Donghaile 2018.

9   Cairnie 2002, 188.

10   Cecil Rhodes is widely known as a symbol of British Colonialism. He was a British businessman, mine owner, politician, and later Prime Minister of the 'Cape Colony' (South Africa). He and his company 'founded' the colonial power 'Rhodesia' (present day Zimbabwe and Zambia) and his actions as a parliamentarian sowed the seeds of apartheid. He was what South Africa History Online (2018) term an 'Arch Colonialist'. See their entry on his life for a good introduction, including discussion of the intersections between Rhodes imperialism, and labour issues.

11   Cairnie 2002, 188.

Positioning this narrative and the problems highlighted above as of a bygone era, would be naïve. For these ironies endure in contemporary narratives of development and rights.[12] They are alive in the statements of heads of state about the origins of nations.[13] They are present in ongoing structures of colonialism.[14] This demands a reckoning with what came before.[15] In Australia and elsewhere, Indigenous leaders point out that their *sovereignty* has *never* been *ceded*, and they emphasise the need to acknowledge what came before, at the same time as what is still here, and never went away.

*

I grew up on stolen land, out in the remote bush in highland Tasmania. In a place where contested property boundaries were guarded by shotguns and colonial era class divisions persisted.[16] Last names mattered, still delineating convict descendent from settler descendent, and revealing those who were newcomers.[17] But the land had a history much longer than colonial history. Folded into the mountain range kooparoonaniara, which separated the highland Big River country from the lowland Northern regions, it was a place where for ten thousand years,[18] ochre was traded amongst the peoples of lutruwita,[19] and where strangers waited on the edges of Country[20] to be invited in. That land is Aboriginal land, but more accurately it's the Country

---

12 Beard 2007; Kothari 2006; Pahuja 2011.

13 For example, Australia's former Prime Minister, Tony Abbot, in 2014 notoriously stated that before British colonialism Australia was 'nothing but bush' and other similar remarks. See Allam 2018.

14 See Wolfe 2006 for conceptualisation of colonialism as a structure not an event; but also read Kauanui 2016, and responses, for important comment.

15 Watson 2009 states, in relation to a legal principle that closes off engagement with the past: 'Can a violent foundation ever grow peace and order? When we examine this skeleton of principle, we will discover a colonial violence that is layered on the broken vertebrae of the past', p. 45.

16 See Hughes 1996, 368–424; Breen 1990, 2000.

17 See Breen 1990; 2000 for discussion and histories.

18 Aboriginal culture and tradition stretch back many more tens of thousands of years. This timeframe marks only migration to the island during the last ice age.

19 The palawa kani (Aboriginal language) name of the island also known as Tasmania. Note: that in this language names are not capitalised.

20 'Country' is an Aboriginal term for land that holds a range of meanings. See Rose 1996; Porter 2018.

of the pallittorre, part of the Northern tribe also perhaps shared with their neighbours the luggermairrernerpairre, of the Big River tribe.

This land on which I grew was also the site of a war to stay in place. pallittorre peoples, who had lived on and shaped the land over thousands of years, such as with practices now recognised as fire management,[21] were pushed off the land from about 1824 onwards[22] and systemic attempts were made to annihilate them, which they fought and resisted.[23] Dispossession was often incredibly violent,[24] the 'black wars' on that land are known as part of a violent genocide.[25] Genocide often justified, and enacted, by settlers through administrative processes, such as land grants, and other colonially allocated rights to land and resources.[26] The ink from some of these processes is still viewable in the basement of the local Land Registry. There, one can find property titles handwritten by a representative of the Crown. Signed. Stamped. Stamped, with the power of the British Empire, signifying recourse to its might. The fence lines, which mark out the land grants that the architects of attempted elimination, like the notorious Governor Arthur, had granted to 'settlers', still criss-cross the landscape.

When I was a child, the kids from the nearby farms would whisper (incorrectly) that 'the name of the mountain means mercy because that's what Aboriginal people shouted when they were driven off the cliffs'. There was some sense of horror in these tellings, for sure, but the tone, and the language employed by the children and adults alike (when they spoke of it) also seemed banal, it positioned an outrageous assertion as common sense, that this was now inalienably, only, *Australia*.

This was akin to that notorious rhetoric of American expansion 'manifest destiny', that claimed divine and everlasting right to an expanding territory.[27]

---

21 See Gammage 2008; Romanin et al. 2016.

22 Breen 1991, 7.

23 Ryan 1996 esp. 'Part II. War: 1826–31' and 83, 139.

24 Breen 2001, 23–31.

25 See Ryan 1996, and on genocide specifically see Tatz 1999, 324.

26 Also, as argued by many part of genocidal processes, see Tatz 1999; Watson 2000.

27 The term manifest destiny was a staple of American expansionist rhetoric for two centuries. This quote is representative: 'our destiny to overspread this entire North America with the almost miraculous progress of our population and power' — Pratt 1927, 798. The term was linked to discourses of racial superiority. See Horseman 1981.

'Manifest destiny' sought to render active dispossession, genocide, invasion, elimination, as simply part of the march of progress, the natural history or foundation of a currently legitimate *state* — both nation state and state of affairs. It was echoed in school textbooks through fleeting mentions of this ten-thousand-year history as a primitive and long forgotten past. The books' illustrations depicted small huddled groups of faded and often nearly faceless people. The teachers described it all as though from an age ago, a shadow, no longer here. There was no mention of war, of administrative violence, of cunning attempts to annihilate people(s). Neither was there any mention of *sovereignty never ceded*, or of ongoing Aboriginal stories or struggles.

It was instead presented to us that disease, against which Indigenous people had little resistance, had emptied the lands of their populations. Even the extent of the existing populations at the time of invasion was denied, and significantly downplayed, with warped statistics serving as another tool to eliminate Indigenous presence.[28] Too weak for the modern world. Such was the march of history, and we were to quickly move on from it. On to the glories of White Australia,[29] the bravery of the underdogs, the wronged convict who 'came good'. The Aboriginal children in those classrooms were told they weren't there anymore. While Indigenous peoples were given only a passing mention, their land, territory, country, resources, property, were even more strikingly, glaringly, absent from these stories. Instead we learned about the battler, the settler, working hard on the land, *their* land. Land earned through labour.[30] Earning property. Productive.

*

But of course they were still there. They are still here. Some of the confidence in this idea of a White Australia[31] seemed unsettled, disturbed, by the land

28 See Watts 2008; Wanhalla 2010.

29 'White Australia' is a term with specific importance as it is related to the 'White Australia Policy' which limited immigration to fair-skinned Europeans for over fifty years, and had an important cultural legacy.

30 A key proviso of understandings of private property in both colonial and liberal democratic systems is the idea of property as created through labour. Sometimes known as Lockean property. See Locke 1690/2014, 17. See Waldon 1990 for discussion.

31 Further to above: it has also been argued that there should be increased scrutiny into the ways that indigenous dispossession and whiteness as racial identity are intertwined. See Moreton-Robinson 2015.

rights case bought by Eddie Mabo to the Supreme Court at the end of the 1980s. TV coverage of this case often bought up longer histories of resistance, and survival.[32] It brought questions of the foundations of Australia into the consciousness of those around me. Questions of votes and representation were raised, of land rights, of law and legal representation, of property, ownership, and theft — it became broadly understood that a crucial foundation of Australian law was a fantastical legal doctrine.

I learned, through our television set and the conversations of adults around me, that this doctrine was a blatant fiction called *terra nullius*,[33] which in Latin means 'land that belongs to no-one'. *Terra nullius*,[34] which was overturned in the Mabo case, had been taken up across many contexts and conquests in the colonial era. It had been used to clear legal space for the inscription of land across the world into imperial domain, and legal jurisdiction. The concept had also been used to uphold a particular conceptualisation of property rights. A Lockean concept, linking property rights to productive labour and use, to rational man, and to the contractual liberal state. This combination has been a key part of White Australia's refusal of Aboriginal land claims.[35]

In a place where invasion and frontier wars were very nearly in living memory, and certainly in recent oral history, such a doctrine showed a lie, a manipulation. And it seemed during the time of the Mabo case that, as its workings began to be revealed, they began to unravel. A particular kind of sovereignty over territory, established through empire, came into public view. Showing the complicity of law with the brute power of imperialism as allowing a twisting of reality. This seemed elusive, cunning, monstrous, able to remove whatever it chose from its own terms of reference. Such as claiming habited lands to be uninhabited, or declaring land to be not land, and not Country,[36] but abstract property.

The depiction of such shifting legal illusions as foundations of political authority, agreed to by citizens or subjects, is fundamental to the modern liberal state. This state has often been called Leviathan.

---

32 In particular the 'Wave Hill walk off' and the fight for citizenship in the 1960s.

33 The history of the use of *terra nullius* has, since Mabo, been extensively researched. There is ongoing debate about whether it should be classified as a legal doctrine. This is returned to below.

34 Rowse 2001.

35 Moreton-Robinson 2007, 2.

36 See footnote on 'Country' above. Rose 1996; Porter 2018.

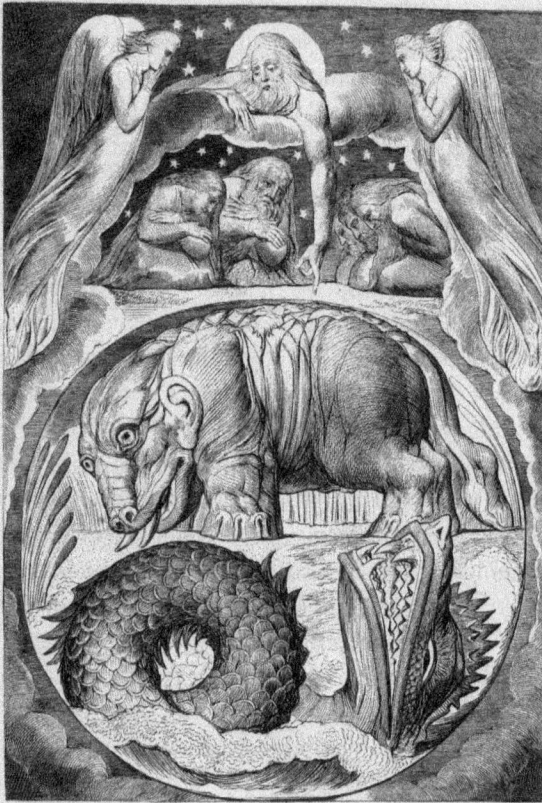

Figure 5. 'Behemoth and Leviathan', by William Blake.

The Generation of Leviathan

Who can open the doors of his face? His teeth are terrible round about. His scales are his pride, shut up together as with a close seal. One is near to the another, that no air can come between them. [...] they stick together, that they cannot be sundered. [...] He esteemeth iron as straw, and brass as rotten wood. The arrow cannot make him flee: slingstones are turned with him into stubble [...] He maketh the deep to boil like a pot.[37]

Leviathan is enduringly enmeshed in Judeo-Christian, Modern, Western, histories and imaginaries, and ways of knowing the world. It is variously conceived as a whale, sea monster dragon, or devil. Interpretations are most often allegorical, metaphorical, but they also range from earnest, to absurd. The cryptozoologist Karl Shukar, who searches for living mythical creatures, posits pseudo-scientifically that the monster is inspired by sightings of Mosasaurs.[38] He is not the first to try to identify Leviathans and many historical texts turn, and return again, to the origins, forms, and identification of the biblical Leviathan.[39]

A foremost trait of Leviathan is that it is powerful and compelling, beyond our comprehension, and elusive, often submerged, or hidden. Yet at the same time we yearn to know and explain it, and identify our appropriate relation to it. This trait speaks to a tension between that which we regard as a foundational or immovable force, such as Leviathan itself or its biblical partner Behemoth, or an abstraction like 'the golden rule' — of treating others as oneself (which is said to transcend cultures). And that which we believe we are able to influence or to transform, that which is considered within the realm of our influence, and society. The terrain created by this particular tension has long been the subject of inquiries into law and politics, particularly in the 'Western' tradition.

Such inquiry has been fascinated, obsessed even, with identifying a solid foundation upon which to comprehend, locate, and justify legal power: political power, the power of the state, power situated in gender relations, power exerted over a group, *et cetera*. Achieving this would settle and put

37 Job 41:14–31, King James Version (KJV).
38 Shukar 1996.
39 For extended discussion of these historical interpretations and excavations see Kinnier Wilson 1975, 3–4.

beyond contention any questions regarding the legitimacy of this power. And this is most readily achieved when those foundations are hidden.

Perhaps the most prominent philosopher of the liberal tradition, Emmanuel Kant, declared uncompromisingly that while *authority* was open to be challenged in defence of liberty, the fundamental underpinning *power* of a political authority must never be questioned, nor even bought into view.

> The origin of the supreme political power, for all practical purposes, is *not discoverable* by the people who are subject to it. In other words the subject *ought not* indulge in *speculations* about its origin with a view to acting upon them, as if its right to be obeyed were open to doubt (*ius controversum*). Whether in fact an actual contract originally proceeded their submission to the state's authority (*pactum subjectionis civilis*), whether the power came first and the law only appeared after it, or whether they ought to have followed this order — these are completely futile arguments for a people which is already subject to civil law, and they constitute a menace to the state.[40]

Herewith we witness the conjuring of something powerful, legitimate, and shrouded. Leviathan helps me traverse this terrain of sovereignty and justice, and in due course will help me ask who benefits, and who is even permitted to exist. But my companion is difficult to apprehend.

> Can you pull in Leviathan with a fishhook or tie down its tongue with a rope? [...] If you lay a hand on it, you will remember the struggle and never do it again! Any hope of subduing it is false; the mere sight of it is overpowering. No one is fierce enough to rouse it. [...] It makes the depths churn like a boiling caldron and stirs up the sea like a pot of ointment. It leaves a glistening wake behind it. [...] Nothing on earth is its equal — a creature without fear. It looks down on all that are haughty; it is king over all that are proud.[41]

Like another monster on which this book will conclude, Leviathan is *undefeatable*. In most accounts, it does not even acknowledge the existence

---

40 Kant 1991, 143 (emphasis in original).
41 Job 41:1–34 New International Version (NIV).

of its assailants. Humans and their humanity are irrelevant to it, and at most might just be swept along in its wake.

It is often a submerged and unknowable force, not conquerable, and to be feared, emanating from a nature of which humans are not able to comprehend.[42] In the biblical story that introduces Leviathan to the Western canon, Job learns that the world is unjust but that God is powerful: He (God) is even able to tame the great Leviathan. Job must trust in God's love even though his suffering is manifestly unfair in relation to his deeds in life. Job's friends, on the other hand, are chastised by God for their assumption that his suffering must be the workings of some sort of divine justice, that Job must have sinned to suffer. Instead there is no justice in this account that can be comprehended by humanity. Power resides solely in the divine, and in divine command. Attempts by humans to explain, or understand justice are depicted as not only absurd but as undermining God's authority.[43] This Leviathan, of course, cannot be compelled, or known, or measured by humans.

Flipping this, yet maintaining the powerful horror, the classic anarchist text *Against His-Story; Against Leviathan!* Perlman[44] instead conjures Leviathan as a stand in, a moniker, for civilisation. It is a book that gave a name (and perhaps a loose form or direction) to the movement known as *anarcho-primitivism*. In it, civilisation Leviathan is a monstrous, masculinist terror...an enduring, yet ever-changing, shape-shifting imposition on freedom and possibilities for freedom present in a more natural and enduring reality. This civilisation Leviathan, instead of representing nature and a struggle with it, forecloses planetary futures, forecloses nature, and, as humans are part of nature, threatens human freedom and life.

The polemical text depicts monstrous successions of civilisation Leviathan(s) in different, metamorphosing forms that have promoted classes, social divisions, professional armies, and nationalisms. All of these annihilate peoples and, in concert, consume the earth with an ever more rapacious appetite.

This Leviathan as civilisation/s is drawing on the *Leviathan* of Hobbes. That Leviathan that lives in and is enacted to legitimise sovereign forms of political authority, and has also become a widespread moniker for the sovereign state.

---

42 See Doak 2014 for discussion of nature and the self in the biblical passages on Leviathan.

43 For well-regarded analysis, see Newsom 2009.

44 Perlman 1983.

This enduringly popular use is certainly not devoid of the biblical and mythical monstrosity described above. A recent instantiation of this is to be observed in the 2014 Russian film *Leviathan*, directed by Andrey Zvyagintsev. The story centres on a character — Nicolai — whose life has been torn apart by the expropriation of his land by the state, which worked in cahoots with the church. Much comment on the picture, which was highly acclaimed at Cannes film festival, centres the character's battle with corrupt people working under the auspices of their institutions. 'Western' press for example situated the film as a brave challenge to the non-liberal Russian state.[45] Much Russian press coverage situated it likewise, but in a negative light. According to the minister for culture *Leviathan* provides a false narrative and problematic depiction of Russian society,[46] and the Orthodox Church hoped to have it banned.[47] But Leviathan in this film is also tied up with land, territory, and time in other ways. According to film historian Julia Vassilieva the movie deals with more than the state or church,

> [L]and is a central issue in the film. It is Nicolai's land that functions as a motor of the story; its prized position on the edge of the cape is what sparks the Mayor's desire to acquire it, and it is Nicolai's ancestral connection to the land that drives him into a self-destructive opposition to state power.[48]

Leviathan then, as the moniker, and the imagery (in this film huge landscapes, whale carcasses on wide-angle deserted shorelines, grim weather, huge skies are foregrounded) is taken up to engage with this complex terrain of state, religion, authority, territory, place, community, and individuality.[49] This Leviathan is also harking back to an established tradition in political thought most concerned with a scientific analysis of the workings of political power, attempting to render political and social power knowable, measurable, and predictable.

Leviathan, as a representation of the sovereign state, was famously bestowed by seventeenth-century political philosopher Thomas Hobbes

45 Bradshaw; Walker 2014; MacFarquhar 2015.
46 Roddy 2014.
47 RT News 2015.
48 Vassilieva 2018.
49 Dargis 2014.

(1588–1679). His use of the monster's name as the title of his book, which charted his at-the-time controversial political philosophy, earned him the nickname 'the Monster of Malmsbury'. Hobbes, his book *Leviathan*, and his use of a monstrous name has been widely analysed.[50] But whatever his motivations there are certain established aspects of Hobbes's monster that are crucial to understanding my companion in this chapter.

In his text *Leviathan or The Matter, Forme and Power of a Common-Wealth Ecclesiasticall and Civil*, Hobbes presented an argument that necessitated a supreme authority — a sovereign — to protect humans from a 'state of nature' that was brutal. Hobbes aimed to convince his reader of a framework of political authority and order based in objective reality, and one that was entirely more valid than those arrived at by the prevailing discourses of the time, which were religious or in the tradition of reasoning and argument. As pointed out by Stillman,

> Only the fiat of a historically real sovereign stands between Hobbes' text and a universal political discourse.[51] [...] His writing is committed to perform for us (and ultimately I will argue, to have us perform) a transformation of metaphor into logic — a transformation, it should be stressed from the start, that aims at a strangely magical event, the incarnation of sovereign power.[52]

Hobbes, in many senses, was attempting to kill the biblical Leviathan, replacing it with a new Leviathan. His relationship with monstrosity and metaphor is complicated, and it is argued by many, including by himself in his writing, that he used the metaphors of monstrosity in order to destroy them. Through his use of (what he saw as) natural laws and principles, the text *Leviathan* makes the case that all argument and reason are but mere opinion, thus creating monstrosities and falsehoods. He instead asserts that true (and natural) political authority arises out of the necessary natural laws and conditions of human existence.

---

50 For introduction, see McFarlane 2018; Lloyd and Sreedhar 2018; for interpretation see Hampton 1988; Stillman 1995; Boucher 2018; *Hobbes Studies* is a high-quality dedicated journal.

51 Stillman 1995b, 151.

52 Stillman 1995a, 799–800.

For Hobbes, life was 'nasty, brutish, and short', and made up of individuals following their passions in ways that led to a state of all-encompassing 'warre of all against all'. Peace was sought and found by handing over authority to a sovereign. In Hobbes, the sovereign's legitimacy and existence, then, was a product of this, and dependent upon it. This symbiotic relationship, based on the fear of the state of war, and constituting sovereignty, was described by Hobbes as a covenant.

> I Authorize and give up my Right of Governing my selfe, to this Man, or to his Assembly of men, on this condition, that thou give up thy Right to him, and Authorise all his Actions in like manner. This done, the Multitude so united in one Person, is called a common-wealth, in latine civitas. This is the Generation of that leviathan, or rather (to speake more reverently) of that Mortall God, to which we owe under the Immortal God, our peace and defence.[53]

Hobbes's work has been credited with the birth of liberalism, and the great secularisation of European thought. It is considered part of a crucial step in the split from church to state, and in the direction of liberal rights. He has often been called the 'founder of modern political philosophy'.[54] Since Hobbes, the monster Leviathan, as moniker for the state, has been ubiquitous in Western political theory. Furthermore, the idea that political power and sovereignty was derived from the agreement of subjects, and later citizens, to submit to power in return for protections of the state has been influential to an extent that is hard to overstate.

In Leviathan We Trust

From the time of Hobbes to the time of World War II, Europe was firmly entrenched in a system of nation states that held enormous power, both over their own territories and across the globe. This age of state sovereignty, inaugurated by the 'Treaty of Westphalia', came to shape the world and its

---

53 Hobbes 1651/1904, Part II, Chapter 17, 118–19.
54 A quote originating with Strauss 1936/1963, viii, but often repeated in the literature on Hobbes.

political institutions. An 'international realm', and international law,[55] came increasingly into being, but these rested on the mythology of national sovereignty. The realities of domination and idealism that this engendered and represented also came to create terrible human misery through the depredations of nationalism so manifest in the Holocaust and the 'great wars'.

Couched in part as a response to this, another powerful liberal/libertarian narrative took hold across the globe; market fundamentalism was increasingly presented as an antidote to the monster of the state, to the social contract of Leviathan. It proposed another kind of foundation, another authority, a naturalisation, not of the state, but with perhaps just as elusive a beast, 'the market'. In this narrative, this other monster of modernity was claimed to provide the only alternative to submitting to the inevitable tyranny and poverty of the nation state Leviathan.

Instead of social contracts that build political orders, like monarchies and states, the market turned on the capacity of contracts to foster something else greater than their sum. But like Hobbes's state of nature, it was also set to the backdrop of a fearful and violent pre-legal reality. An adversarial reality where, because anyone could potentially steal or pillage at any time, banding together through legal agreement to foster greater security, especially of claims to property (and rights to exclude others from it) is essential. Secure contracts, agreements, promises, property rights, foster *trust*. Trust in transactions and exchange. This trust in turn enables smooth exchange, efficiency, and innovation. This trust, and security, created by contracts and the policing of them, is seen to create wealthy prosperous societies, and peace. And such peace would be most realisable where the government retreated (so the story goes) to as small as possible, and got 'out of the way' of those pursuing progress, assuming only the role of the nightwatchman. A 'neoliberal state' that was almost utopian.

But the market does not slay Leviathan nor dampen its purchase on our political imaginary, for they are elusively entwined. Loïc Wacquant, French-American social theorist, and a student of the sociologist Pierre Bourdieu, invokes Leviathan in his description of the neoliberal state. He describes a state invested in a 'roll-back' of welfare, and other forms of social provision, and a 'roll-out' of the penal arms of state power, of what he terms 'prisonfare'.[56]

---

55 Sovereignty meaning: 'supreme authority within a territory'. See Besson 2011 (for general overview); see Anghie 2007 (for critical history).

56 Wacquant 2010.

The growing penality of the poor by the state, and the remaking of the state in a newly monstrous form is tied, in this depiction, to growing social insecurity. This insecurity caused not by actual increases in criminal behaviour, but following from the state's remaking of itself in the image of the market fundamentalism with which neoliberalism is synonymous. This move from welfare to 'prisonfare' is achieved through tropes of individual responsibility, through positioning the poor as deficient and responsible for their poverty. It is tied up with the 'prison industrial complex'. Neoliberal Leviathan 'punishes the poor' and renders them criminal in order to maintain its legitimacy as it vacates the spaces of social provision and welfare.

This work shows the neoliberal Leviathan as very much out and about and *at work* in the world. It poses in America, for example, as protector of the 'good' white middle classes against the terrible criminality of the racialised and criminalised poor. It penalises poverty to hide the complicity of the state's 'bureaucratic field' in the production of poverty. Wacquant states that 'A diligent carceral system is not a deviation from, but a constituent component of, the neoliberal Leviathan'.[57] In this sense the state which claims to give over power to the market, to the individual, that claims to be a nightwatchman, is no less Leviathan-like, no less massive, and no less monstrous.

> We live in capitalism, its power seems inescapable — but then, so did the divine right of kings.[58]

Other recent invocations of Leviathan depict a state in rapid flux, deeply tied into transnational constructions of international, global, regional, and local order. Tied up in complex economies and alliances, and characterised by ever changing borders and contestations of territory and jurisdiction. The American political historian Charles Maier, for example, conjures Leviathan in the title of his work *Leviathan 2:0, Inventing Modern Statehood*.[59] In the text he argues that around the 1850s a new form of state emerged. His analysis challenges orthodoxies that see the state as emerging in a European context, around the time of the Treaty of Westphalia, and then *progressively* spreading across the world. Modern statehood should instead be conceived as a global

---

57 Wacquant 2010, 197.
58 Le Guin 2014.
59 Maier 2014.

phenomenon, and as a relatively recent and — more likely in a new era of globalisation — fleeting iteration of political/territorial power.

The existence of a Leviathan commanding absolute sovereignty in Hobbes's era should not be overstated, according to Maier. He explains instead that empires, from the Mughal Empire, to the British Raj, to the Chinese imperial domain, accepted various kinds of 'partial sovereignty' within their domains, with kings, princes, sultans and rajas practising sovereign power over people and territory.[60] These domains were complicated too by religious authority, and its crossing of boundaries and borders. So, while absolutely tied up with imperial power and colonial expansion, the modern state was not a progressive expansion, but emerged in many places simultaneously, in for example Mexico, Japan, China, and Europe, as recently as the 1850s.

This modern state, furthermore, was, according to Maier, possible not only owing to the workings of a natural political order, as in Hobbes's Leviathan. It was also made possible due to the expansion of new communicative and military capacity. A new era of statehood, and the creation of societies defined by the state, was inaugurated by those who *both* formed the political structures of statehood, and controlled powerful new technologies (trains, rapid fire guns, telegraphs, and so on).[61] Although related, this should, according to Maier be conceived of as a new Leviathan, rather than a simple continuation of older forms of political authority.

Maier argues, further, that in this era of Leviathan 2.0, 'the states won, expanded, and then turned with murderous single-mindedness on each other and sometimes their own citizens'.[62] Modern states, globally, drove people(s) resistant to their increasingly dominant authority into the margins. Margins, both in regard to location (highlands, swamplands, remote areas which trains and other technologies couldn't reach, or control easily), and also in regard to their status within, or in relation to the state,[63] through for example, citizenship, or property ownership. This Leviathan grabbed power through

---

60 Ibid., 9.
61 Ibid., 1–14.
62 Ibid., 13.
63 Ibid., 2–14.

domination and war that was located everywhere, internal, external, and at the borderlands, all at the same time.[64]

This is reflective of other important work in the study of states, their margins, the people excluded from them, and the horrors perpetrated by them. In *Modernity and the Holocaust*,[65] Polish sociologist Zygmunt Bauman argues that to understand the Holocaust as an anomaly, or as only rooted in older ethnic, or tribal, rivalries or feelings of rivalry, is problematic. Instead the particular logics of the modern state, the emphasis on machine-like and careful scientific planning, the exacting of 'solutions' to problems of the state, can be seen to have actively enabled the horrors of the Holocaust. It can be seen, he argues, in this respect, as a product of modernity and not anathema to it.

Patrick Wolfe, too, explains how the technologies of expansion in the American frontier, and their logics, should not be positioned as stateless, lawless activities. He argues that 'rather than something separate from or running counter to the colonial state, the murderous activities of the frontier rabble constitute its principal means of expansion'.[66] These murderous logics were not always present in just the military apparatus or through genocidal or warlike activities, though. As noted above, they were also administrative including the remaking of land as property, and the inscription of law that aims to annihilate or eliminate already existing relations to place, or as societies.[67]

Aspects of the logics within these processes are evident in Hobbes's *Leviathan* as well. Many have argued that Hobbes's depiction of the 'state of nature' as brutal and violent is directly related to the positioning of some societies as 'pre-political', as in a state of anarchy. In turn, contributing to a conceptualisation of law and statehood that denied indigenous peoples a claim to sovereignty.[68] Indeed throughout the work *Leviathan* there are depictions of 'American savagery', that refer to Native American peoples, which are used to describe the 'state of war' against which the civil body must be contrasted.[69]

---

64 In Britain contentious recent laws requiring landlords to evict undocumented tenants mean that migrants experience 'a border in every street', and reflect a current iteration of this condition.

65 Bauman 2000.

66 Wolfe 2006, 392.

67 Ibid., throughout text.

68 Maloney 2011, 189.

69 Moffit and Sebastian 1996, 284–85.

According to monster theorist Nicholas Robbins, in *Leviathan* Hobbes 'envisions humans transcending their monstrous nature by incorporating themselves within the mechanical body of Leviathan,' asking 'his audience to exchange one form of hybridic monstrosity, the ancient wolf-man, for another, the modern man-machine'.[70] This is also evidenced in Hobbes's use of the wolf-man trope elsewhere than the text of *Leviathan*.

But Hobbes is not the only one to deploy this kind of imagery. Such depictions have served in building other depictions of sovereignty, as discussed by philosopher Jacques Derrida in a series of lectures titled the 'The Beast and the Sovereign'.[71] In these lectures Derrida demonstrates that throughout modern European history there has been a persistent association between animals and beasts, and sovereignty. From monstrous tropes, as in Hobbes's wolf and Leviathan, to stately princes depicted as foxes in Machiavelli.[72] Derrida explains (by drawing on Hobbes's assertion in *Leviathan* that sovereignty is simply not possible as a covenant with God or beasts) that the discourse of beasts is used because, like animals or gods, the Sovereign is also positioned as beyond, and outside, of the law.[73]

This positioning, like Kant's positioning of power, is also reflected in international law, where the international realm is depicted as a system of sovereign states outside of which is pure anarchy. However, many see the post-war international order, ostensibly based on an ideal of respect between equal sovereign states, and their differences, as caught up in continuing colonial projects that are transnational and embedded in the processes of international law, and development, despite, and even utilising narratives of sovereignty and statehood.[74] International law scholar Jenny Beard for example, presents the compelling argument that the institutions of international law, and development bought into being in the post-war era — the era of supposed 'decolonisation' — in fact aimed to remake the world within certain visions of development and progress that were deeply tied into liberal, and Christian, mythologies.[75]

70 Robbins 2014, 103.
71 Derrida 2009.
72 Machiavelli 1961.
73 Derrida 2009, 55.
74 Anghie 2007; Pahuja 2011.
75 Beard 2007.

So, while the ideal of state sovereignty in international law is that of a bounded, independent civil and political authority, it is in practice varied, and caught up in local, imperial, and global iterations of power and authority.[76] In *The Islamic Leviathan: Islam and the Making of State Power*,[77] international studies scholar Seyyed Vali Reza Nasr demonstrates the role of religion in state formation in the 'Muslim world' [sic]. He shows how in both Pakistan, and Malaysia, Islamization has been used to significantly increase the power of the state Leviathan. This resonates with other work on the Malaysian state too, some of which demonstrates the ways in which iconography and rhetoric of Islam and Modernity, tied into a global imaginary, are bought together to consolidate state power. Bolstering a particular ethnically inflected Leviathan, but not an isolated one, instead always related to a global stage.[78]

Many of the above discussions engage with new consolidations, and forms, of state power, of Leviathan's authority. Others still, engage the ways that political, economic, and legal/regulatory power increasingly seeps into regions, changing scales of authority, potentially undermining, or circumventing, states. Extensive work has shown how since the 1970s new political economies have taken material and productive relations (in particular the relations of capitalist enclosure, production, and accumulation) beyond the nation state, or into agglomerations (locations of intensified capitalist production and accumulation, usually big cities).[79] A range of new, and renewed, scales of authority that transcend borders have become important to understand.

Some highlight the ways that these changing scales of political economic relations, commonly understood as economic globalisation, also combine with expanding communicative technologies and complex cultural flows to fundamentally change the way that power and authority work.[80] This may include, for example, the ways that cities create networks that are cross-border,

76 Darian Smith 2013.

77 Nasr 2001.

78 Lee 2014; Bunnel 1999; Yeoh 2005.

79 Harvey 1989 'Time-Space Compression', and 'The Transformative and Speculative Logic of Capital'; and 2001: 'Globalisation and the "Spatial Fix"' in which he describes: 'capitalism's insatiable drive to resolve its inner crisis tendencies by geographical expansion and geographical restructuring', p. 24.

80 Appadurai 1996; Sassen 2008; and see especially Darian-Smith 2013 and Massey 2007.

and in turn leave their regions and localities behind in economic terms, or in alliances such as the 'C40' network to combat climate change.[81] Or how globally connected social movements, such as those represented in the World Social Forum, mobilise across borders.[82] Overall, there is a broad consensus that 'it is not possible to take the geo-political boundaries of the nation state as a given, nor view states as discrete and autonomous legal units operating within international, transnational or global domains'.[83] That there are instead complex global-to-local permutations of law and authority in the making.

A recent text entitled *Leviathan Undone*[84] engages aspects of this context. It brings together a range of work from the early 2000s that muses on new complex iterations of *scale* in a globalised, highly interconnected, world. Chapters in the book show that while states must be taken seriously there are new loci, and scales, of power, influence, and authority, and asks if Leviathan is undone, what might emerge? In a paper from 2013 titled 'Raising the Regional Leviathan' Jonathan Metzger engages this, but posits the making of new Leviathans. Inquiring into the ways in which regions form new political, spatial zones (and using an example from Northern Europe) he contends that new 'publics' can and are being born and becoming more stabilised. These regions have what he calls 'stakeholder communities' that come together to create new Leviathans, and should be seen as 'publics in the making'.[85] In this sense Metzger positions stakeholder communities, as caught up in new Leviathan-like social contractual relations, but he departs from older Leviathans as the new iterations are without the state.

In Your Name

One place that a similar Leviathan, based in a stakeholder frame is increasingly manifest is in recent pushes for corporate social contracts. Contractual models of business ethics in the field of corporate social responsibility are increasingly widespread.[86] These models of ethics, and models of doing business are

---

81 Fraundorfer 2017; and see Landau-Ward 2017 for an overview of changing spatial politics of cities.

82 Steger and Wilson 2012.

83 Darian-Smith 2013, 9.

84 Keil and Mahon 2010.

85 Ibid., 1368.

86 See especially Donaldson and Dunfee 1999; 2002.

often posited with aspirations that traverse the globe, and aim to transcend or complement state-centric political order. Interestingly, corporations are increasingly compelled by states, who are hoping to withdraw responsibility from the social realm, to foster corporate social responsibility arrangements with communities in order to legitimise their operations.[87] Often, corporate interests and entities are required by governments (elected or otherwise) to foster social contractual models of ethics, to follow the unsaid principles of Corporate Social Responsibility, yet at the same time such activities are also in other senses left unlegislated, and unregulated. This creates a complex set of social contractual relations that ties into global, local, and national realms.[88]

One example of this is the growing popularity of the idea of 'social licence to operate'. An increasingly prevalent form of engagement between extractive industries and the communities in which they work, it has become accepted as a necessary part of extractive operations globally.[89] According to a study conducted in 2017 'after mentioning the concept of social license in less than 10 articles a year from 1997 through 2002, news media mentioned social license in more than 1,000 articles a year from 2013 to 2015, and more than 2,000 articles in 2016'.[90] In this model a social contract with communities is seen as an increasingly essential part of all extractive operations. As such, considerable resources and efforts are allocated (by corporate interests) to foster and obtain such a 'licence'.

The aim, at its most basic, is to 'advance a business case' in a socially acceptable way — in order to enable the company's operations. This is generally achieved through a framework where all stakeholders are mapped out and expected to benefit. The company in question, which will already have an official licence to conduct operations granted by the state, or local authority, will often employ consultants to obtain a social licence.[91] These consultants, or other actors, aim to create the foundations of a new social contract through community consultation, group meetings, and research into local dynamics. This is always a contract framed in the terms of furthering the interests of those involved. It is deeply imbued in a reduction of questions to the identification of self-interested actors (stakeholders) whose interests

87 Frynas and Stephens 2015, 484.

88 Ibid.

89 UongoziInstitute 2018; Moffat and Zhang 2014, 61.

90 Gehman et al. 2017, 293.

91 UongoziInstitute 2018 from 5:40.

and conflict must be reconciled through the forging of what is often termed a 'micro-social contract'.[92] We might see this as the making of a Leviathan. This model is firmly based in the contractarian tradition that provides legitimacy, and authority, *through social contract*. But it's not a contract tied into global justice, or even established, local, ways of being lawful. Like older Leviathans questions of justice are possible *only after the Leviathan*. Like other Leviathans there is no recourse to refusal within this frame, indeed, corporate interests are known to be extremely reticent to consider that social licence might include a serious consideration of community consent, and in practice it doesn't.[93] So, while the orthodoxy in the consultancy world is that it is too risky to operate without a social licence (because such operations will be subject to protests, direct action, disruption),[94] the 'getting' of a social licence is always the aim of the process, it isn't an open question. There is no scope not to consent to operations. A 2012 study reflects this, stating that 'our analysis has revealed, the contemporary application of social licence is more about reducing overt opposition to industry than it is about engagement'.[95]

The spread of the social licence model is, in large part, a reaction to both grassroots and transnational protests and resistance that challenged a range of unethical actions and disastrous outcomes connected to the operations of multinational corporations in the 1980s and 1990s.[96] These protests often railed against the complicity of corporates, elites, and states in the exploitation of communities and their means of subsistence, or cultural heritage, particularly in regard to mining and forestry operations. Such injustices led both to globally reaching protests and boycotts, as well as to transnational court cases across a range of jurisdictions.[97] Questions of environmental and social justice came to the fore.

However, questions of environmental and social justice wedded to extractive industries have scope and implications well beyond the auspices of the social contractual domains assumed in the social licence to operate model.

---

92 Wilburn and Wilburn 2011, 9–10.

93 Slack 2008.

94 UongoziInstitute 2018, 3:30–4:00.

95 Owen and Kemp 2012, 6.

96 See Prno and Slocombe 2012 for analysis of the origins of social licence to operate.

97 The case of Shell in Nigeria over the execution of local activist Ken Saro-Wiwa, which was tried in a US court, before being settled out of court, is perhaps the most well known. See Manby 2016.

Even if the most stringent aspirations for social licence are met, there is also something lost, including the ability for local peoples' ontologies and relations to land and place to be respected.[98] Furthermore, there are ongoing questions of justice as the actions of extractive industries impact many locales, including those removed from their operations. In our global critical condition, just as the production of an iPhone in Shenzhen, or its consumption in Hong-Kong, impacts the life chances of villagers around Coltan mines in Sudan, so too does the extraction of fossil fuels, oil in Nigeria, Australian coal, or Canadian oil sands. All these impact the lives of those affected first through massive changes in weather patterns and sea level rises, such as dwellers on Pacific islands who call for climate justice.[99] Furthermore, a social contract enabling extractive operations in place, concentrated on a stakeholder frame, may exclude and therefore eliminate other possibilities for local peoples to resist, or refuse operations.

In this way creating new Leviathans to justify local extractive operations may present newly monstrous justifications, legitimised through a recourse to self-interest and social contract. New Leviathans. New ways in which Leviathan may continue to contribute to the elimination of ways of living, and being, that don't fit within its bounded, contractual, authority.

Between the Devil and the Deep Blue Sea

Indeed, Leviathan is always tied up with justice. Following along behind Leviathan in this text we have explored the terrain of law and authority through contractual relations and, as we have seen, this idea has been highly influential. It is even foundational to many legal and political contexts around the world. But according to Huemer,

> Most modern hypothetical contract theories are meant to explain something broader than political authority. Typically, they aim to account for the part of morality that concerns, in the words of Scanlon (1998 7), what we owe to each other.[100]

---

98 Ehrnström-Fuentes and Kröger 2017, throughout and 355; see also Moffat and
     Zhang 2014, 69.

99 350.org 2017.

100 Huemer 2013, 36.

Moral and political philosophy in the 'Western' tradition does have a long history of considering contracts and contractual relations as the basis for political and social authority. While this stretches back to Aristotle and Socrates, post-Hobbes's *Leviathan*, the idea of the social contract has been a cornerstone of much political science and theory. The moral and political philosophers who rely on some form of social contract to underpin their theorising are said to be in the 'contractarian' tradition and have included Rousseau, Kant, and more recently Rawls and Gauthier.[101] And while 'the traditional claim that individuals have consented to the state cannot plausibly be defended, hypothetical social contract theorists turn instead to the claim that individuals would consent to the state under certain hypothetical conditions'.[102]

However, as has been explored above, a *contractual* understanding of sovereignty, combined with 'a unified supreme authority, territorial integrity, and individual rights'[103] has also been tied up with colonial terror and expansion. It has contributed to the creation of marginalised populations, internally, externally, and the *elimination* of other forms of society and territory, of other sovereignties,[104] which have been driven off cliffs and pushed into the borderlands. And rather than freeing people, as the free market vision of society would have it, contracts have been argued by writers such as Carol Pateman,[105] Charles W. Mills,[106] and Virginia Held,[107] as tying subjects into relations of domination and exploitation.

These iniquitous relations may be gender-based, as in marriage contracts which, according to Pateman, tie women into patriarchal relations. This links into another older, feminist, critique of social contracts that can be traced back at least as far as Mary Wollstonecraft Shelley, and is a central theme in her

---

101 Cudd and Eftekhari 2018.

102 Huemer 2013, 36. Note: this idea is used by Kant in the defence of his position on foundations discussed in the first part of this chapter.

103 Moreton-Robinson 2007, 2.

104 It is important to add, although beyond the scope of this text, that indigenous sovereignties, and experimentations with sovereignty should be differentiated form this liberal form. See Moreton-Robinson for excellent discussion.

105 Pateman 1989; see also Pateman and Mills 2007.

106 Mills 1997; see also Pateman and Mills 2007.

107 Held 1987; 1993.

book *Frankenstein*.[108] This critique highlights the exclusions created by social contracts. Who, and what, is considered human? Who is party to the contract, and who can't be? And what inhumane acts does this exclusion justify? And enjoin? Many feminists have argued that the liberal individual at the centre of all the major social contract theories is conceptualised in a form representative of an economic agent — masculine, European, and productive, without care responsibilities.[109]

C. W. Mills's 1997 influential book *The Racial Contract* also takes up, and then extends, some of these critiques. Overall, he argues that more important than the social contract in Western society has been the racial contract. This contract has, throughout modern history, determined who is counted as a full person, and in turn who is counted as sub-human, and as such whose land and bodies are open to theft and exploitation. Mills uses many examples from throughout the world, and the colonial era, to demonstrate a very real, live contract, explicitly visible in administrative and legal apparatus, and documentation. These instruments and apparatus consolidated whiteness as a racial contract, and, through a depiction of brownness, as other than human, enabled the justifications of white superiority and racism that, in turn, enabled exploitation across, within, and at borders, along the lines of race. In this way he demonstrates how contractual relations can operate on a scale beyond the state with real consequence.[110]

Other kinds of contracts can do this kind of work as well. In a recent analysis of the working of land registration systems in Australia, Sarah Keenan traces the ways in which land titles named 'Torrens Titles' which were based on shipping contracts, can reproduce times and places of colonialism and whiteness.[111] I recall those enduring criss-cross fences of my childhood stamped out in colonial registries offices, and meting out an administrative denial of pallittorre sovereignty. Keenan argues that these can 'hold up' ongoing systems of settler-colonialism, and produce and maintain them into new futures, like time machines.

108 For discussion of this see Beenstock 2015.
109 See especially Held 1993, and her conceptualisation of 'economic man'.
110 Mills 1997.
111 Keenan 2017.

An Act of State

In Australia the doctrine of *terra nullius* turned out not to have been a consistent, or uncontested legal doctrine at all. Yet it remains powerful. Instead of consistency it can be seen to have been made and remade in the Australian courts over time.[112] Indeed, it was remade across the breadth of the British Empire over four hundred years. Crucial changes in interpretation and effect emerged in different times and places, when it was taken up to justify imperialism in Africa for example, as compared to when it was used to justify ownership of the polar regions.[113] It was sometimes used to *hold up* state sovereignty, but sometimes confined to the justification of property rights despite or prior to state sovereignty.[114] Both of these iterations, however, were taken up to justify colonial dominion. This leads some to assert that *terra nullius* should be understood as the *product* of an 'attitude' or a 'cultural disposition'.[115] An established practice of meaning reflected in law, that, like 'manifest destiny', positioned the dispossession of indigenous peoples as a *fait accompli*. Or as a logic or discourse that, like Hobbes's *state of nature* (so crucial to the social contract) helped to position some people as savages and others as civilised.[116]

In the Mabo decision, the judges are known to have explicitly rejected *terra nullius* as an anachronism. But the key judge, Justice Brennan, instead brought into his decision, what has been called an 'Act of State'.[117] The purpose of this was to ensure that no Aboriginal claim to land could undermine the skeletal principles of Australia, and its legal authority, based in sovereignty.[118] Some argue that this 'Act of State' did similar work to *terra nullius*, in that it still claimed to have the power to extinguish Aboriginal claims to land and territory, Aboriginal law, and sovereignty, and to justify the sovereignty of Australia.[119] This is despite the law, culture, and sovereignty, that both came before and is still here. This is certainly a reification of the nation state Leviathan, but

112 Falk and Martin 2007.

113 Fitzmaurice 2007, 10–13 and throughout.

114 Ibid.

115 Ibid., 14.

116 Buchan and Heath 2006.

117 Falk and Martin 2007.

118 Mabo v. Queensland (2) 1992.

119 Watson, 2002, 186, 191–92; Buchan and Heath 2006.

it is also tied into the broader practices of contractual liberal ways of being, and justifying authority, such as those that render some ways of being as pre-legal, and primitive, and others as sovereign and legitimate. So, a practice of *terra nullius* still persists, rather than a singular identifiable, legal, doctrine. We might ask then, how and where does it manifest? Does it meet with the new Leviathans we've discussed here as well, and do they (re)produce it?

Leviathan's Wake

Political and legal authority produced through social contracts aims to create a form, a Leviathan, that is foundational, and bounded. That which is *within it* is subject to its authority, while that which is *without it*, or *before it*, does not matter to it, and is open to elimination, exploitation, or unfettered use. What came before it is often positioned as undesirable, or primitive. Furthermore, although bounded (in the sense of having a boundary, a border), Leviathan is not static. It is able to define and redefine the foundations and borders it requires, reflexively. It can do this as much in relation to structures of power (whiteness, nation, profit, the state) as to any scientific, objective, or cultural truth or territory. And, as this Leviathan is embroiled in globalisation it is revealed, as both an apparition and an elusive yet monstrously important presence. A presence that crosses some borders while maintaining others.

We might perhaps see glimpses of contractual authority as trails in Leviathan's wake. Elusive iterations of sovereignty, social contract theory, individualism, narratives of civilisation and savages, and of the 'state of nature'. These building blocks of Hobbes's Leviathan might disappear, be submerged, into the grey areas between states and markets and social movements. Yet, at the same time they will resurface and reappear, remaining as logics of rule and political authority, of importance in our global critical condition. While they are not in themselves Leviathans, through them Leviathans may emerge.

We might be careful then, not to assume that Leviathan is just alive in the state, or in ever-renewing populist leaders with their eye-catching slogans and loud nation-building rhetoric. Nor should we only see Leviathan as alive in the visions of market fundamentalist utopians in their pin-striped suits of armour, or their new, neoliberal Leviathans. Lest we forget to also look into the iterations of contractualism and sovereignty that traverse these orders.

Leviathan might be related instead to 'the devil in the detail', manifesting through legal and 'ethical' codes, and practices, rather than, or as well as, economic orders, nation states, or kings. Here, as elsewhere, the generation of Leviathan may be best observed between the lines, and where spoken of in whispers.

VI

Is Alien to Predator as Nature Is to Culture?

IT WAS SUPPOSED TO BE A SHORT LITERATURE REVIEW FOR AN ARTICLE. That review should have examined some of the literature around States' efforts to control sexual behaviour and give a concise answer to the question I was asking. I, Julian, asked myself, why would a State try to regulate people's sexual activity at all? Although an answer to that question might seem obvious to others, it wasn't to me, and I struggled to get to the root of it. The outcome of that struggle was my book, *Policing Sexuality: Sex, Society, and the State.*[1]

In revisiting that book, I was surprised to find that there was an author whose ideas were influential but whose name seldom appears. That author is Sherry B. Ortner, and she has explored the fundamental bases of gender inequalities across societies. For example, in her essay, 'The Virgin and the State,'[2] Ortner suggests that because 'one's sister or daughter is potentially a wife or consort of a king or nobleman', families will attempt to make them worthy of this, and their virginity or chastity is better at symbolising this worthiness than beauty, because 'virginity is a symbol of exclusiveness and inaccessibility, nonavailability to the general masses, something, in short, that is elite'.[3] Although in reality 'the whole business is terribly complex,'[4] in short,

---

1 Lee 2011.
2 Ortner 1978.
3 Ibid., 32.
4 Ibid., 26.

with the rise of States, 'for first time the term patriarchy becomes applicable' and women are 'brought under direct and systematic control'.[5] However, it is another better-known essay of hers that I will be exploring in detail in this chapter. I first shared these ideas with undergraduate students in 2010, in a circumstance that I didn't realise at the time was one of tragedy.

In July that year I sat in my office in the Malaysian campus of an Australian university and received a call from a student. The student told me that their lecturer had not arrived to deliver the first lecture of that semester's film class. It had been over a quarter-of-an-hour since class ought to have started and the students weren't sure what to do. I said I would try to locate my colleague and that I would come over to the lecture theatre presently. As I walked the short distance, he didn't answer his mobile phone. I could not have known then that later that day I would be accompanying the Malaysian police as they broke down the door to his apartment, in which he had passed away the night before.

Instead, I assumed that he hadn't realised semester had started. I apologised to the class and explained that I was sure that things would be back to normal next week. However, before dismissing them, I attempted to ensure that the students' time wasn't wasted. I had in the months before that day completed the manuscript for *Policing Sexuality*, and so questions about gender and sexuality remained on my mind. Because of my research with activists and because I regularly wrote articles for a Malaysian magazine, I often tried to think of accessible ways to convey academic ideas, such as those relating to gender and sexuality. A monster film I had happened to watch recently seemed to capture perfectly the kinds of gender dynamics that Ortner had described, and so I delivered an impromptu lecture that used this film to explore issues of gender and sexuality.

I began by saying that the medium of film was an important one through which society reflects and explores itself, and that through film we can come to better appreciations of what it is to be human, and the issues that humanity faces. Great films have the ability to make diverse aspects of the human condition more apparent and accessible, and to wrestle with humanity's conundrums. However, the film that I went on to discuss with them was far from an example of a 'great' film. In fact, it was a B-grade sci-fi film that has been credited with ruining what is surely one of the great monsters of recent times,[6] the Xenomorph Alien which was first seen in Ridley Scott's 1979 movie

5   Ibid., 25.
6   E.g., Denham 2015.

Alien. The lamented movie in question was the 2004 film *Alien vs Predator*, directed by Paul W. S. Anderson. I explained that this much-maligned film was able to speak to the question of the universal subordination of women by men, and that I would explore the film with them through the ideas of Ortner in her classic essay 'Is Female to Male as Nature Is to Culture?', which has been read by countless undergraduate students around the world (and which is better known than 'The Virgin and the State'). I told the class that Ortner's interpretation of the socio-cultural relationships between males, females, nature and culture are mirrored in the movie *Alien vs Predator* (*AvP*). In *AvP*, the alien species known as Alien, from the series of four sci-fi-horror movies starring Sigourney Weaver, is female and the embodiment of *nature* (*Alien*, 1979; *Aliens*, 1986; *Alien³*, 1992; *Alien Resurrection*, 1997). The alien species known as Predator, from the series of two movies starring first, Arnold Schwarzenegger (*Predator*, 1987), and second, Danny Glover (*Predator 2*, 1990), is male and the embodiment of *culture*. Despite being a B-grade movie, *AvP* was a vehicle for understanding Ortner's argument in 'Is Female to Male', which rests on the idea that 'women are seen as closer to nature than men, men being seen as more unequivocally occupying the high ground of culture'. She goes on to say that because 'culture' is seen as superior to 'nature', men have come to occupy superior positions in society over women.[7]

However, I concluded by noting that Ortner's work and *AvP* were not only useful in understanding gender relations. I outlined to them — as I will do for you in this chapter — that they also shed light on the rhetoric around 'The War on Terror' which followed the 9/11 attacks in the US. But first...

Alien Is to Nature...

The Xenomorph, which first appeared in *Alien* in 1972, is a thoroughly sexualised monster. Harvey R. Greenberg wrote that movie's alien creature is 'one of the most frightening monsters ever brought to the screen'. He goes on to describe it as '*mysteriously ungraspable, viciously implacable, improbably beautiful*, and *lewd*'.[8] Speaking of the original 1979 movie, John L. Cobbs declares that 'What Alien is about is gestation and birth' with the film's logo being 'the cracked alien "egg" about to "give birth" to the horror within'.[9]

---

7   Ortner 1974, 84.

8   Greenberg 1986, 93; emphasis original.

9   Cobbs 1990, 198–99.

The association of the Alien species with reproduction, indeed rampant unrestrained reproduction, remains important in all the Alien movies, but especially so in *Aliens* and *AvP*.

Alien, as Stephen Mulhall has pointed out, is the epitome of nature. He writes that

> the alien species appears not so much to follow nature's imperatives as to incarnate them. This is not because it is driven to survive and reproduce, but rather because it is so purely driven, because it appears to have no other drives — no desire to communicate, no culture, no modes of play or pleasure or industry other than those necessitated by its own continuation as a species.[10]

As I explained to my colleague's class, at no point in the lifecycle of the Alien species in any of the movies do Aliens undergo any socialisation or enculturation. All that the Alien has by way of intelligence and weaponry is that with which it is born. Its behavioural repertoire may be regarded as instinctual. Although Aliens communicate with each other, they do not possess language. Certainly, the short period of their lives captured in *AvP* precludes language learning. Their vocalisations are reminiscent of birds or, at best, dolphins. According to the neuroscientist, Terence Deacon,[11] neither can be regarded as comparable to human language.

The Alien species goes through three developmental phases which are morphologically distinct. These phases are the egg phase, the face-hugger nymph phase, then the mature phase which begins with the initially diminutive chest-burster which grows into its adult form. These three phases are reminiscent of the lifecycle of flies, frogs, and jellyfish.

Socially and in terms of their lifecycles, there are similarities between Aliens and termites. In *AvP*, as in *Aliens*, there is one enormous queen which ceaselessly lays eggs from an immense egg-producing sac. Then there are any number of smaller non-reproducing 'workers' whose job, it seems, is to find food in which nymph Aliens can pupate.

The Alien species, then, is manifestly both the epitome of nature and, because the activities of the queen and the workers alike are dedicated to

---

10 Mulhall 2002, 18–19.

11 Deacon 1997.

the end of reproduction, they are also evidently female. Worker termites are, incidentally, sterile females.

This association of females with nature, according to Ortner, is extant in human cultures. Ortner argues that there are three main reasons why this is so. The first of these is that the woman's body and its functions involve her more in the reproduction of the species, thus placing her closer to nature. Drawing on the work of Simone de Beauvoir's *The Second Sex*, Ortner points out that much of the female body serves not the benefit of the individual woman, but the egg and its maturation. In pregnancy, vitamin and mineral resources are channelled to the foetus at the expense of the woman, and childbirth is dangerous to her. Breasts are of no relevance to the woman's own health and menstruation is often painful and bothersome. The female, according to de Beauvoir as quoted by Ortner, 'is more enslaved to the species than the male, her animality is more manifest'.[12]

The second of Ortner's three reasons is that women's social roles are also seen as closer to nature than men's. Like all mammals, a woman's body generates milk for consumption by a baby and the mother–child relationship is seen as natural. Young children require supervision and that it is the mother who should take this supervisory role seems natural, because she is already nursing another child, or because it is seen as an extension of her nursing role. Children are themselves closely associated with nature — they crawl, excrete without control, and cannot speak.[13] A woman's role in the early socialisation of children, bringing them from animality to humanity, places her situation somewhere between the realms of nature and culture, and, on that scale, closer to nature.

Drawing on the contribution by Nancy Chodorow to the same volume as Ortner's paper, Ortner offers her last reason. The woman's psyche is closer to nature than men's. Men, it is suggested, are regarded as more 'objective and inclined to relate in terms of relatively abstract categories, women more subjective and inclined to relate in terms of relatively concrete phenomena'.[14] The difference in psyches are not inherent, but rather the result of socialisation. A son must model his masculine identity after a father who is usually more remote than the mother. This involves an identification with the (abstract) *position* of the father, rather than a (concrete) personal identification with

12 Ortner 1974, 74.

13 Ibid., 78.

14 Ibid., 81.

an individual. The daughter, in developing her feminine identity, need only persist with the existing and present relationship with her mother, and not abstractly-defined characteristics. Women therefore 'enter in relationships with the world that culture might see as being more "like nature" — immanent and embedded in things as given — than "like culture" — transcending and transforming things through the superimposition of abstract categories and transpersonal values'.[15] Thus, women again are seen as closer to nature and men closer to culture.

...as Predator Is to Culture

Predators are humanoid, tall, and muscular. They are evidently coded male, with bodies that possess male bodybuilders' muscular chests and slender hips. Actions such as chest-beating and gladiatorial fist-pumping confirm their masculinity. We know from the preceding *Predator* movies that the Predators are hunters. They make use of space travel and sophisticated weaponry and armoury.

AvP is set almost entirely within a pyramid complex built by the Predator species, deep below the surface of Antarctica. The premise of the movie is that satellites owned by Weyland Corporation discover a giant pyramid two thousand feet beneath the Antarctic. Billionaire Charles Bishop Weyland recruits a team of various experts to be the first to explore this pyramid. Satellite images reveal that the pyramid shares characteristics of Aztec, Cambodian, and Egyptian pyramids implying a common and ancient derivation.

Most of the recruits descend into the pyramid through a tunnel they discover and which, it is declared, 'no team and no machine in the world' could have made. There, the exploration team discovers a complex pyramid structure adorned with hieroglyphics and art. In the course of the film, we discover through the main characters a number of things about the Predators. One is that other pyramids in the world were built using knowledge bestowed on humans by Predators. The Predators taught the humans how to build and were worshipped by the humans as gods. Every hundred years the hunters returned and demanded human sacrifices which they used to 'breed the ultimate prey' — namely the Alien species. The Predators then battled the mature Aliens to prove themselves worthy of carrying 'the mark'. This mark is made on a Predator's own forehead using the corrosive blood of a vanquished

15 Ibid., 82.

Figure 6. Image from the film Alien vs Predator (2004).

Alien. Should the Predators fail to conquer the Aliens, however, the Predators ensured nothing survived by detonating an all-destroying explosive.

As the human explorers move through the pyramid, they trigger a mechanism that results in the defrosting of a frozen and static Alien queen that is bound in chains. Immediately, the helpless Alien queen begins to lay eggs directly onto a conveyor. (The connections that can be made here between enslaved female reproductivity and masculine industrial modernity are almost too obvious to point out.) Later and elsewhere, one part of the exploration crew of humans finds an ornately marked chest that the archaeologist in the team manages to open. Inside are three guns, like the laser-guided shoulder-mounted cannons seen on Predators in the preceding movies. The humans take these and in doing so set off another mechanism that shifts the internal configuration of the pyramid every ten minutes. As a result of these reconfigurations, the human team becomes split up and is gradually picked off by Aliens that have emerged from the chests of other unfortunate members of the exploration team.

That the guns were removed from the chest was not part of the Predator plan and three novitiate Predators attempt to retrieve their guns from the humans. The three Predators, large as they may be, nevertheless rely on their technology to kill the Aliens. They have particular need of the guns in the hands of the explorers. While they attempt to acquire them, two of the three Predators are killed by Aliens. Meanwhile all but two of the humans, a female explorer and a male archaeologist, have also been killed. These two humans who are carrying the last gun realise that if the Alien species reaches the Earth's surface they could wipe out all life there. Thus, the two humans decide to try to return the gun to the remaining Predator. In the course of so doing, the archaeologist is killed, but the last human gives the gun to the Predator and also forms an alliance with it. Together, they destroy the nest of eggs and all the Aliens, although the Predator dies as it slays the queen which escaped to the surface.

Is Alien to Predator as Nature Is to Culture?

Whereas the Alien species is nature incarnate, the Predator species, owing to its advanced technology and the allusion that they may in fact be the source of humanity's culture and technology, is culture incarnate. According to Ortner, it is 'through the medium of technology and symbols' that the male, 'lacking natural creative functions, must (or has the opportunity to) assert his creativity externally, "artificially."[16] In the context of *AvP*, it is only through its culture and technology that Predators can defeat the Aliens and thereby adorn themselves with 'the mark' and so complete a biologically unnecessary but culturally imperative rite of passage. Indeed, as anthropologist Roy Rappaport stresses, ritual is 'the social act basic to humanity'.[17] That is, it is the act that raises us (and Predators) above animality.

Ortner asserts that it is through the performance of ritual that the distinction between nature and culture is wrought. She notes that most cultures have initiation rites and that these are primarily for boys. These rituals 'move the child ritually from a less than fully human state into full participation in society and culture'.[18]

The ritual transition of Predators to adulthood does not mark a biological transition, but rather a social and abstract one. A hypothetical biologist unfamiliar with Predators would not find any significant morphological differences in pre and post initiation specimens. The same biologist would find, however, great differences between nymph and mature Aliens. The reason that the transition of Predators through the stages of life is marked by ceremony, while the transition of Aliens is not, is precisely because the transition amongst Predators requires a symbolic event to mark the transition — the transition is not biological, it is symbolic. But ritual is not merely symbolic, according to Mary Douglas; ritual actually brings about the required changes at the social level.[19] In accord with Ortner's thesis, then, Predators, representing both culture and maleness, are operating in the realms of the symbolic and abstract, while Aliens, representing nature and femaleness, are operating in the concrete.

With culture, argues Ortner, humans manipulate and assert control over nature and it is through the performance of ritual that the distinction between nature and culture is made.[20] Drawing on de Beauvoir, Ortner notes that the transcendental nature of hunting and killing, which are male activities, confers more prestige than birth. Although none-the-less evidently part of culture, women, owing to their bodily involvement in reproduction, are 'intermediate between culture and nature, lower on the scale of transcendence than

16 Ibid., 75.
17 Rappaport 1999, 31.
18 Ortner 1974, 76.
19 Douglas 1970, 302.
20 Ortner 1974, 84.

men'.[21] Men thus occupy 'the high ground of culture' more certainly, and use culture and technology to transcend and control nature. Claude Lévi-Strauss expounds upon the implicit association between women and animal species. He notes that both are

> subject to the same type of beliefs and practices since in the eyes of culture, they have the common feature that man has the power to control and increase them. Consequently, men by cultural means exchange women who perpetuate these same men by natural means and they claim to perpetuate species by cultural means and exchange them *sub specie naturae*, in the form of food-stuffs which are substitutable for each other since they all provide nourishment and since, as with women also, a man can satisfy himself by means of some foods and go without others in so far as any women or any foods are equally suitable to achieve the ends of procreation or subsistence.[22]

The generative function of women, compared to the killing activities of men, accords men greater prestige. And whereas the Alien species only behaves in accord with biology's basic four imperatives — feeding, fighting, fleeing, and reproduction — the Predator species also engages in sport. The first thing that the three Predators do when they arrive on earth is to hunt down and string up the humans who remained on the surface. Their armour is adorned with skulls and other trophies of previous hunts. Ortner writes that,

> Within de Beauvoir's framework, we realize it is not the killing that is the relevant and valued aspect of hunting and warfare; rather, it is the transcendental (social, cultural) nature of these activities, as opposed to the naturalness of the process of birth, [quoting de Beauvoir] 'For it is not in giving life but risking life that man is raised above the animal; that is why superiority has been accorded in humanity not to the sex that brings forth but to that which kills'.[23]

21 Ibid., 76.
22 Lévi-Strauss 1966, 125.
23 Ortner 1974, 75.

This reading of *AvP* can be extended in a number of directions to comment on issues of gender, capitalism, and modernity. But it is perhaps in violence and war, as I explained to my colleague's film class, and in gendered processes of dehumanisation, that its relevance is most apparent. The politics and rhetoric of the globally divisive 'War on Terror' reflects *AvP* and Ortner's ideas too well.

Is Orient to Occident as Alien Is to Predator as Nature Is to Culture?

'It is commonly acknowledged', writes Harvey R. Greenberg, 'that the science-fiction and horror genres often provide an exquisitely sensitive index of disruptive social pressures'.[24] As such, Greenberg sees that the movie *Alien* 'invokes rationales called up by dominant groups throughout history to label those of other nationality or creed, caste or color "inhuman"'.[25] Similarly, Jan Mair notes that 'In science fiction, the "other" as "alien" is deployed to concretise the deeply divisive dichotomies of race and gender embedded in the repressive structures and relations of dominance and subordination'. 'Hollywood films' she continues, 'must have an enemy, an evil "Foreign Other" in order to galvanise rampant jingoism'.[26] She goes on to point out that the threat of Communism 'has been conveniently transferred to the fear of the Middle East (Arab/Islam)' and that 'Our erstwhile neo-alien, the demonised "Vicious Oriental"/Arab is mythologised into the concrete ontological entity that threatens the very future and existence of humankind'.[27] One may assume that given that her book chapter was published in 2002 and that Mair does not mention Osama bin Laden, that she wrote prior to 11 September 2001 and so missed the ascent of Osama bin Laden as primary global Bad Guy in the period following 9/11.

The attribution of blame for the 11 September 2001 attack by the US and the characterisations of the attack's culprit recapitulated entrenched figurations of the Oriental/Arab world in comparison and in relationship to the Occidental/West. These figurations contain definite parallels with Ortner's thesis, especially when viewed through the prism of *AvP*. The Others here are

24 Greenberg 1988, 166.
25 Ibid., 170.
26 Mair 2002, 35.
27 Ibid., 38.

Osama bin Laden and the Muslim/Arab world on the one side with the Alien species, and the US and the Occident on the other side with the Predator.

The figuration of the relationship that the Occident has with the Orient is most famously advanced by Edward W. Said in *Orientalism*. According to Said, 'Orientalist generalizations about the Arabs are very detailed when it comes to itemizing Arab characteristics critically, far less so when it comes to analysing Arab strengths. The Arab family, Arab rhetoric, the Arab character, despite copious descriptions by the Orientalist, appear de-natured, without human potency'.[28] The 'singular avoidance' of Oriental literature by new American social-science, according to Said, has had the net effect of emasculating and dehumanising the Arab/Islamic Orient in modern American awareness.[29] What the Orientalist discourse implies is that 'what is really left to the Arab after all is said and done is an undifferentiated sexual drive'.[30] Thus, the non-cultured and de(human)-natured Arab 'produces himself, endlessly, sexually, and little else' and that 'the only way in which Arabs count is as mere biological beings, institutionally, politically, culturally they are nil, or next to nil'.[31]

We see in Said's figuration that the place of the Orient vis-à-vis the Occident is highly congruent with the place of the Alien species vis-à-vis the Predator species. That is, Alien is without culture as such and in essence little more than generative biological drives. The metaphoric emasculation of the Orient through the ignoring of its cultural achievements thus also places it closer to femaleness.[32]

The relationship of the Predator species with the Alien species in *AvP* also mirrored the relationship of the US/the Coalition of the Willing, with Osama bin Laden/Islamic terrorists in the speeches of George W. Bush and in the Western media. In particular, just as the Predator hunts the Alien and destroys its nest, so too did the US hunt Osama bin Laden and desire to destroy al Qaeda. Speaking of the US's enemies, George W. Bush said, 'we hunt an enemy that hides in shadows and caves'.[33] Continuing with the hunting theme, he said, 'they will try to hide, they will try to avoid the United States and our allies — but we're not going to let them. They run to the hills; they find holes to get in.

28 Said 1995, 310.
29 Ibid., 291.
30 Ibid., 311.
31 Ibid., 312.
32 See also Said 2004, 217.
33 Bush 2001a.

And we will do whatever it takes to smoke them out and get them running, and we'll get them'.[34]

However, perhaps most arresting for its resonance with *AvP* is *Time* magazine's portrayal of the American military and its enemy in Afghanistan.

> The hunters stalked their prey from the sky and in the shadows, armed with instruments of death and waiting for Osama bin Laden to reveal himself. Above the gnarled ridges outside the besieged cities of Jalalabad and Kandahar, U.S. warplanes unloaded laser-guided Maverick missiles and 5,000-lb. bunker busters to collapse limestone redoubts and bury anyone taking cover inside. Members of the U.S. Army's clandestine 800-man Delta Force tracked likely bin Laden hideouts, equipped with night-vision goggles and stun grenades, in case they had to creep inside the mountains, and laser pointers, in the hope that they could get warplanes to do the dirty, risky work.
>
> [...]
>
> With hunters closing in, he [Osama bin Laden] was said to be moving nightly among caves in the honeycombed mountains stretching from Jalalabad to the northern half of the Uruzgan province. American F-15Es, unmanned Predator drones and commando ground troops killed scores of Taliban and al-Qaeda lieutenants.[35]

While the US army is 'picking up bin Laden's scent' with sophisticated technology, including unmanned Predator drones, and killing scores of Taliban and al Qaeda personnel, *Time* reports that Pakistani intelligence believes that al Qaeda survivors, to evade the US Army, would likely 'lodge themselves in narrow canyons among the summits, near dried riverbeds shielded from American pilots by boulders and shadows'. The enemy then, is reduced to animal-like methods to evade the hyper-sophisticated US army, thus completing the Predator-technology-male-hunter-Ego/Alien-nature-female-quarry-Other division.

---

34 Bush 2001b.
35 Ratnesar 2001.

Speaking of another war article in *Time* magazine in 1999 which reported on violence in Sierra Leone, anthropologist Michael Jackson noted the lack of humanising perpetrators of violence and seeing their actions in a historical context.

> [N]othing in the *Time* story helps us understand the social and historical background to the war. Rather than point out that the rebellion is a response to decades of corruption and misrule by a succession of State governments and military juntas, the collapse of patrimonialism, and struggle by marginalised Sierra Leone youth for a stake in their nation's immense wealth, *Time* has recourse to time-honoured Western stereotypes of African primitivism.[36]

The rhetoric of categorical difference, he goes on to say,

> disguises the violence that has accompanied the exploitation of Sierra Leone's mineral wealth by foreign corporations in direct collaboration with local elites over a period of thirty years, and overlooks the impoverishment, frustration, and disempowerment that are the very condition of the possibility of the emergence of 'demented' and 'drug-addled' mobs in a nation where, as one non-plussed emergency-relief specialist put it, 'extreme violence is not characteristic'.[37]

The fear is that any attempt at understanding the violent Other will seem to legitimise the violence. Meanwhile, failing to understand contexts and portraying the Other in dehumanised terms invites, as Hariz illustrates in the following chapter, an exterminatory response if the dehumanisation of the Other is effective. The sentiments towards al Qaeda and the Taliban of some Americans who wanted to 'wipe Afghanistan off the map' remind us of the attempted destruction of the Alien species and its nest in *AvP* and *Aliens* (whose depiction in these films sublimates the horror and misery of human-against-human war, and whose sublimation is a vehicle with which film lecturers and critics alike approach aspects of human existence too unpalatable to directly assail.) The exterminatory reaction is one which we also have towards pests,

36 Jackson 2002, 134.
37 Ibid.

whose pathological reproductivity provokes our attempt to annihilate them. What thus seems to be in evidence in *AvP* and in the War on Terror discourse is, as Ortner has drawn our attention to, a constellation of ideas in which females and the feminised Other are too easily attributed sub-human status by a masculinised and enculturated self. If they are not being harnessed, they are to be destroyed.

Figure 7. 'Srebrenica', by Adis Elias Fejzić.

VII

Vampires and Ratko Mladić:
Balkan Monsters and the
Monstering of People

THE BALKANS, A REGION IN SOUTHEAST EUROPE TO WHICH BOSNIA-
Herzegovina (hereafter 'Bosnia') belongs, abounds with different types of
monsters and many related myths and stories. Here, in Bosnia and this chapter,
are monsters in humans and humans as monsters that have traversed from
the primordial epochs into the popular imagination and become infamous
symbols of the modern Balkans. These monsters are not cute; what makes
them frightening is that their monstrosity was real.

Being born there, I, Hariz, grew up with the Balkan monster stories that
still can instil a real fear deep in my bones. The most widely known monsters
associated with this part of the world are vampires, with Count Dracula
becoming almost a symbol of the dark, wild, and brutal Balkans. The name
of the Balkans itself, originating in the Turkish language and meaning 'a
mountain chain', has often been used as a pejorative term from which words
such as 'balkanisation', 'balkanise', and 'balkanising' are derived to describe
neighbourly hostility, fragmentation of territory, and cruel violence.[1] At least
in part, such ideas about the region stem from longstanding Western phantasies
about the Balkans as a kind of liminal space nested between the Orient (or

---

1   Hirsch, Kett, and Trefil 2002.

Byzantines and Islam) and the Occident (or Europe and Christianity).[2] As Maria Todorova describes in her seminal work *Imagining the Balkans*, the region has been seen as Europe's 'Orient', the 'other', a geographic and cultural entity which is either outside or on the edge of European civilisation; becoming a synonym for reversion to the tribal, the backward, the primitive, and the barbarian.[3] Phantasies about bloodthirsty vampires roaming through the region, soaked in darkness of the strange, the unknown, and the exotic, were reinforced by popular movies made in the West, especially several versions of the Dracula films originally based on the novel written by Bram Stoker in 1897.[4] As with many other stories in the Balkans, the most famous Balkan aristocrat, Count Dracula, was a historical figure. Vlad III Dracula lived between 1428 and 1476 in present-day Romania and is remembered as a cruel ruler of Wallachia and a brutal military leader, which earned him the nickname Vlad the Impaler.[5] However, local folk tales — and indeed history itself — comprise many other 'vampires' and many other 'monsters' that, like Dracula, are not just a product of popular imagination and primordial superstition.

Monstrosities of similar and different kinds to those of Vlad Dracula have been frequently attributed to the region, including those taking place in recent history. Many in some form or another relate back to the Ottoman period. Some five centuries of Ottoman rule in the Balkans, under which many aspects of arts, culture, and architecture flourished, are often reduced to the proverbial 'Turkish yoke', that is, the cruelty of the Turks against those they kept occupied.[6] Some of those reductionist narratives have gained mythical proportions and have been utilised for nation-building and nationalistic agendas.[7] One such case is Serbian nationalism, in which the real and imagined battles against the Ottomans have come to symbolise the modern Serb nation,[8] while the term 'Turk' has become a synonym for Serbian enemies, the Muslims of the Balkans: Bosniaks, Albanians, and other ethnic groups that

2   West 1941; Bakic-Hayden 1995; Wolff 1994.

3   Todorova 1993.

4   Vrbančić and Božić and Vrbančić 2011; Perić and Pletenac 2015.

5   McNally and Florescu 1994.

6   Buturović 2015; Boose 2002.

7   Jezernik 2004.

8   Anzulović 1999; Jakica 2010.

at various stages in history adopted the Islamic faith.[9] In this process, popular narratives dealing with the encounter with and resistance to the Turks, turned some local historical figures into villains and monsters, while others became superheroes.

Writing about the Balkan Monsters

Over three decades the Balkans have remained stuck in the old narratives and continue to be associated with political instability, fragmentation, exclusive forms of ethno-nationalism, and ethnic violence. The series of wars that were fought during the 1990s in the former Yugoslavia continue to dominate day-to-day politics in the region and the perception of the region from the outside. Often, these stereotypes are exploited by local politicians in the region to justify their policies in a very similar fashion to how the same stereotypes were utilised at the height of the conflicts during the 1990s.[10]

At the time, the negative images about the Balkans provided a basis for the interpretation and justification of the violent break-up of the former Yugoslavia, among which 'ethnic cleansing' and genocide in Bosnia were its most brutal episodes. One prominent example of such essentialising narratives of the war and the region, read as widely by international policymakers as by lay audiences, is Robert Kaplan's book *Balkan Ghosts*, written in the style of a historical travelogue. Here, the author described the Balkans as a region dominated by ethnic conflicts, poverty, and endemic hatred. Kaplan reduced the whole history of the region to 'a long, desperate compromise with a succession of invaders, marred by decades of Turkish rule, Nazism and Communism'. The book unapologetically promoted the thesis about ancient hatreds as the main cause for the hostilities and wars in the region. Kaplan went as far as to argue that 'Nazism can claim Balkan origins', speculating that 'among the flophouses of Vienna, a breeding ground of ethnic resentments close to the southern Slavic world, Hitler learned to hate so infectiously'.[11] Focusing on the events of real and fictional violence that took place in the region in distant and recent times, while ignoring that similar and indeed much more brutal violence has been a part of European history, Kaplan offered an essentialist narrative about the Balkans and its monsters — or ghosts as he

---

9   Sells 1996.

10   Halilovich and Phipps 2015.

11   Kaplan 1993, xxiii.

called them — that were made of ordinary 'Balkanites' of different ethnic and religious backgrounds.[12] Portraying the rich cultural diversity in the region as a source of conflict and recalling the assassination of Franz Ferdinand in Sarajevo in 1914, which triggered the First World War, he suggested that the Balkans was an ideal place to start a global conflict. He thus offered yet another scary narrative about these Balkan monsters to a Western audience.

The Utility of the 'Ancient Hatred' Thesis

Unfortunately for the Bosnian civilians who became the main targets of the brutal military aggression in 1992, Kaplan's book became an influential source of pseudo-historical knowledge about the assumed primordial ethnic savagery in the Balkans for many policymakers and commentators in Western Europe and the USA in the early 1990s. They understood the war in Bosnia as bona fide evidence for this thesis and as a natural course of events that could neither be prevented nor rationally explained. Some critics of Kaplan argued that after reading the book, the U.S. president Bill Clinton became very hesitant to intervene in the conflict and risk placing U.S. troops in Bosnia.[13] This significantly prolonged the war and gave sufficient time to the monsters in charge of the modern military weaponry to advance their campaign of 'primordial violence' in Bosnia, resulting in the killing of tens of thousands of people: men, women, and children.

The civilised Westerners — embodied, among others, in the European Union negotiators Lord Owen and Lord Carrington and the United Nations commander, the Canadian General Mackenzie — who were tasked with stopping the bloodshed in Bosnia, were rather impressed by the efficiency of the modern Balkan 'vampires' and their skill at spilling the blood of hundreds and thousands of civilians in broad daylight in the streets of Sarajevo and other Bosnian towns with unpronounceable Balkan names, such as Goražde, Bihać, Žepa, Srebrenica, and so on. The myths about powerful monsters and cyclical violence occurring in the region resulted in these and other important Western players developing a certain dreadful respect and admiration for the perpetrators, instead of empathising with their victims. To tame the monsters, Lords Owen and Carrington advocated for 'peace plans' that would reward the perpetrators by accepting their crimes as legitimate means of gaining control

12 Halilovich, 2013.
13 Drew 1995.

over the places they erased from the ground.[14] General MacKenzie, who was a frequent guest at the Serb military headquarters and had participated in social events organised by General Mladić, became a fan of the mighty Serb general who could aim his artillery at any civilian target he wanted, without fearing the consequences as the civilian targets did not have firepower to fire back. General MacKenzie, the commander of the UN Peace Keeping Forces in Bosnia, was 'too rational' to confront such 'irrational' violence.[15]

Thanks to the 'ancient hatred thesis', the killings of civilians and war crimes committed by a very modern army and trained officers were perceived by these international representatives and many political commentators, media, policymakers, and the public as being primordial violence and never-ending vengeance that was hard to comprehend and even harder to prevent or stop from happening.[16] Rather than challenging these stereotypes, the Serbian propaganda used such interpretations to its advantage, appropriating them to mask the truth about the Serb military operations aimed against the non-Serb civilians in Bosnia and Croatia and later in Kosovo.[17] It was Serb propaganda that introduced the term 'Turks' for the Bosniaks as well as embracing notions such as 'warring parties', 'people killing each other', and even going as far as to accuse the victims of bombing or killing their own people.[18] For instance, while it was a well-known fact, established by the UN military observers, that only the Serb troops had long-range and heavy artillery, along with military jets and helicopters, and that the only troops besieging other cities in Bosnia were the Serb troops, after every artillery attack and bombardment of civilian targets in the cities of Sarajevo, Tuzla, Goražde, Bihać, or Srebrenica — and sometimes there were thousands of such attacks in a single day — the Serb propaganda would blame the Bosnian 'Muslim extremists' for committing those crimes against themselves in order to provoke 'an international intervention'.[19]

14 Kumar 1997.
15 MacKenzie 1993.
16 Halilovich 2013.
17 Anzulović 1999.
18 Donia 2006.
19 Cigar 1995.

The 'Monster'...

The mastermind of this propaganda as well as Serbian military strategy was general Ratko Mladić, the commander-in-chief of the so-called 'Army of Republika Srpska' (VRS). He personally ordered and oversaw all the major attacks and operations aimed at the besieged Bosnian cities and is responsible for many monstrous crimes, including the crime of all crimes — genocide.[20] However, naming him a 'monster' and 'the butcher of Bosnia', as many commentators have done since 1992, has further 'balkanised' and 'mythicised' the crimes he had committed. It was as if to dehumanise him meant to separate him from the ideology he had served and thanks to which he had been able to thrive as a 'monster', a master of death, a modern-day Vlad Dracula.

Before 1991 he was a largely unknown character outside of the Yugoslav military cadre. Ratko Mladić was born during World War II, in 1943, in a small village near the mountainous Bosnian town of Kalinovnik. His name Ratko derives from the word *rat* which in Slavic languages means war — his name means *warrior* in English. *Nōmen est ōmen*; since his early teenage years, he was groomed to become a soldier, by initially completing a military cadet school in Belgrade and subsequently enrolling in the Yugoslav People's Army (JNA) military academy, where he trained to become an officer. After graduating from the military academy in 1965, he began his professional career in JNA, climbing up the ranks and completing additional military specialisations. The context in which he lived and worked fostered and rewarded his narcissistic and bullying personality. He had the perfect background for someone whose military career was his main identity: he came from a peasant background, his father was killed during World War II, he was a member of the Communist Party, and lastly, he was an ethnic Serb. All these factors contributed to the kind of military officer he was to become. When during the 1980s JNA became increasingly Serbianised, with most non-Serb high officers either being sent into retirement or sidelined into less important posts, Mladić accelerated into higher echelons of the Army. In 1991, at the eve of the dissolution of the Yugoslav Federation, he was appointed to command the JNA corps supporting the Serb rebels in the western part of Croatia, a region which declared succession from Croatia and formed the so-called Serb Republic of Krajina. The creation of the 'Serb Republic' was accompanied by ethnic cleansing of Croats and the destruction of Croatian cities and towns. After successfully accomplishing the task he was given in Croatia, in 1992 Mladić became a key figure in the creation of another 'Serb Republic' in Bosnia and was named the commander of the self-proclaimed Army of Republika Srpska (VRS).

The Croatian author Slavenka Drakulić, whose surname coincidentally derives from the name Drakula, described Mladić in the following words: '[He] is a stocky man with a big head and a bullneck. While he talks in the sharp, imposing voice of someone who is used to issuing commands, his reddish face glistens with sweat. His looks suggest that he enjoys earthly pleasures such as food and drinks'.[21] While this is a fairly accurate description of his looks, it must be added that Mladić did not display any physical anomalies that could define him as a monster. His blue eyes and baby-shaped face gave him a benevolent look. But as many of his victims and those who met him face-to-face learned, this was a monster in disguise, someone who was capable of planning and ordering many small and large monstrosities, including the destruction of a whole people — the crime of genocide.

...and his Victims

Mladić's primary victims were all those who, in any manner, stood in the way of the creation of the mono-ethnic 'Republic' he was to carve out of the multi-ethnic social fabric of Bosnia. However, the troops he was in command of not only killed Bosnian Muslims (Bosniaks) and Bosnian Croats — the main target groups of the Serb 'ethnic cleansing' campaigns — they also killed many Bosnian Serbs, 'Yugoslavs', 'Bosnians', and all others who did not fit the profile of a 'pure' Serb as defined by Mladić and those like him, or who refused to join in what from the beginning was clearly to be a campaign of genocide. At least for much of 1992, when most of the war crimes in Bosnia were committed, the brutal violence against the Bosnian population could hardly be called a war at all. Heavily-armed Serb soldiers and militiamen slaughtering, raping, torturing, and illegally detaining civilians in Bosnian towns and villages was 'one-sided' violence, rather than a war with two armies confronting each other.[22] It was more akin to the eradication of vermin.

Throughout 1991 and in early 1992, to counter growing tensions and talk of a possible war in Bosnia as well as to demand an end to the war in Croatia, Bosnians of all backgrounds organised peace rallies across the

21 Drakulić 2003, 142.
22 Maass 1996.

country, especially in Sarajevo, the cultural and political capital of the country. On 4 April, they staged the largest public meeting in front of the country's Parliament. Many prominent Yugoslav artists took part in what became a series of spontaneous performances and speeches. Thousands of workers left their jobs to say no to war. Students made large banners: 'Make love, not war'. It was a colourful peace parade and the protesters were resolved not to leave until they got assurances from all those in power regionally and internationally that there would not be a war in Bosnia.

As a twenty-two-year-old university student I enthusiastically joined thousands of protesters of all 'ethnic' and other backgrounds at the peace rally. I remember singing 'Give Peace a Chance'... And this is when I was shot at for the first time in my life. In classic terrorist style, bullets were sprayed at us from the surrounding hills and from the tops of buildings where our attackers, the Serb nationalists, took their positions and waited for orders from Mladić 'to start the war'. Thousands of the peace protesters fled in panic. In front of two of my friends and me, an older man was hit by a bullet. We carried him into the nearby Philosophy Faculty building from where he was then taken to hospital. Another two protesters, both women, fellow students Suada Dilberović and Olga Sučić — neither of whom fit into the ethnic or gender categories used to interpret the war in Bosnia — were not so lucky. They both died where they fell. They were the first victims of the Siege of Sarajevo.[23]

For War You Need Two Armies, for Massacres Just One

The fact that none of the protesters at the peace rally were armed — a similar scenario could be seen across Bosnia — only helped Mladić put into action the plan of the 'ethnic unmixing' of a multiethnic society, a society sharing a unique tradition of a pluralist culture and way of life. Mladić knew that he had been given a difficult task which could only be achieved through the most brutal violence, in which he was willing to sacrifice as many of his fellow Serbs as was needed. In one of the first series of artillery attacks on Sarajevo, Mladić disclosed his strategy on the radio: he issued orders to his gunners to aim at the suburbs where 'there weren't many Serb residents'. Not a resident of Sarajevo, this was a random guess by Mladić, as in fact there was not a single part of the city that was not ethnically mixed. But he must have known that

23 Halilovich 2017.

the thousands of shells he was pouring daily down on Sarajevo would not be able to distinguish Serb heads and limbs from the heads and limbs of others.[24] Massacres seen via the media across the globe as they were unfolding were one of the main features of the 1990s wars in the Balkans.[25] Sometimes the war seemed like endless carnage where everyone was massacring each other, 'neighbours killing neighbours' as it was often reported. Such oversimplifications put the victims massacred on the streets of Sarajevo and other besieged towns across Bosnia in the same basket with those who were killing them. However, for anyone who wanted to see the truth, the truth was there. The famous photo taken by Ron Haviv in the Bosnian town of Bijeljina in April 1992, showed very clearly that the 'killing each other' thesis was a misrepresentation: armed men in uniforms were kicking the lifeless bodies of the civilian victims they shot: the perpetrators were the Serb militiamen and the dead civilians were the Bosnian (Muslim) residents of Bijeljina.[26] There were countless similar examples where perpetrators and victims were shown for what they were. However, even the slightest 'confusion' about what was happening in the 'Yugoslav conflicts' was helping the perpetrators of war crimes to increase their deadly activities.

The initial local massacres turned into 'ethnic cleansing', a systematic campaign of violence aimed at killing, intimidating, and expelling the ethnic other from the territories that came under control of the Serbian forces. Nationalist propaganda was a very efficient means of war, playing a role in both inciting the violence and covering up the large-scale atrocities committed against the 'enemy', while inflating — even fabricating — the suffering of their own ethnic group.[27] This in turn was used to justify the need for pre-emptive 'defensive' attacks, most often resulting in the slaughter of civilians.

The devastating fear accompanying the violence was the strategy studied at the JNA military academy called psychological warfare, which was now being tested on (former) Yugoslav citizens. The former military academy graduate General Ratko Mladić showed creativity in taking psychological warfare to a new level. His military strategy involved the deliberate use of excessive violence aimed at giving the war 'uncivilised', 'barbaric', and 'medieval' qualities. The language was adjusted to fit these qualities so that in all formal and informal

---

24 Ibid.

25 Kurspahić 2003.

26 Time 2017.

27 Kurspahić 2003.

communication by Mladić's troops Bosniaks (Bosnian Muslims) were referred as 'Turks', Croats as 'Ustaše', and Albanians as 'Šiptari', all derogatory terms that represented the Serbs' real and imagined enemies from the distant and recent past.[28] As a result of this systematic violence and propaganda, the 1990s wars were often interpreted in 'broader historical contexts' as unfinished battles from the past, most often as a belated episode of the 1389 Kosovo battle.[29]

The Ball of the Vampires

Both the deliberate and spontaneous use of myths, fiction, and folk tales to interpret the events of the 1990s have become integral parts of the narratives about the conflicts. Many researchers, writers, and artists coming from a broad spectrum of disciplines have borrowed from and built upon these narratives to create their own versions of the stories of war and conflict in the Balkans. An innovative approach to tackle the modern monsters of the Balkans and link them to the real historical events was presented by James Lyon, a Balkans historian turned fiction writer. His novel *Kiss of the Butterfly* 'weaves together intricate threads from age-old Balkan folklore and modern events, to create a tapestry of passion and betrayal, obsession and desire, the thirst for life and the hunger for death'.[30] While his book is a work of fiction, it is based on the actual events, some dating back to the fifteenth century, others to the 1990s.[31] Lyon makes connections between the events and links protagonists of those events into a coherent narrative. The main protagonists of these events, as described by Lyon, are vampires, representing the dark side and inflicting suffering on innocent non-vampire folk.

Lyon's book starts with Vlad Dracula and the historical event that took place in 1476, when the Prince of Wallachia committed a massacre in the Bosnian town of Srebrenica. The bloodshed Vlad Dracula caused in the town can be compared with that inflicted by the modern monster, General Mladić, 519 years later. In July 1995, Mladić oversaw Europe's worst massacre since World War II and the first act of genocide proven in an international court.[32]

28 Cigar 1995.
29 Boose 2002.
30 McKinley 2013.
31 Lyon 2006.
32 ICTY 2017; Honig and Both 1997; Cigar 2015.

Rather than supporting the ancient hatred thesis and seeing the bloodshed in the Balkans as endemic to the region, Lyon uses vampire fiction to unveil the real cruelty of political crimes by 'modern vampires': the late Serbian president Slobodan Milošević, who died in jail in The Hague before being sentenced for the war crimes in the Balkans, and his henchmen on the ground; Željko Ražnatović Arkan, the notorious Serbian warlord who was gunned down by his criminal rivals in Belgrade in 2000; General Ratko Mladić, the commander of the 'army' tasked with completing ethnic cleansing and the genocide of the non-Serb population in Bosnia; and Dr Radovan Karadžić, a mad psychiatrist who turned the capital city of Bosnia into his psychodrama experiment using binoculars from the Serb militias positioned like a microscope to observe how killings and destruction affected the behaviour of the subjects he kept under siege. These monstrous 'games' resulted in more than 11,500 deaths in Sarajevo alone, and many times more in other parts of Bosnia.

Srebrenica: Return of the Vampires

For more than four years, Mladić proved that he could undertake new and larger atrocities, earning the title of the Butcher of Bosnia. The butchering culminated in July 1995, when he captured the United Nations Safe Area of Srebrenica, a demilitarised zone in eastern Bosnia. At the time when it was overrun by the Serb forces led by General Ratko Mladić, the UN Safe Area completely depended on the protection of the UN battalion that surrendered to Mladić and handed over the civilian population, which they were responsible for protecting, to Mladić's mercy.[33] In the absence of any other options for survival, tens of thousands of Srebrenica residents and refugees trapped in this last Bosniak enclave in eastern Bosnia either fled into the nearby forests and then tried to reach Bosnian government-controlled territory on foot, some one hundred kilometres away, or ran frantically to the UN compound at Potočari, two kilometres from the town's centre.[34]

Along with tanks and heavily-armed soldiers, General Mladić was also armed with a TV crew, making sure that his 'historic victory' was broadcast as it was unfolding. In one of the tapes, standing in the deserted town square of Srebrenica, the red-faced General was issuing orders to his troops to advance 'on to Potočari', the UN base. He then makes a theatrical pause to make

33 Nuhanović 2007.
34 Honig and Both, 1997; Nuhanović, 2007.

the important statement to the camera and explains how he is 'presenting Srebrenica as a gift to the Serb people', and that what is to follow is 'a revenge upon the Turks'. As previously suggested, naming his victims 'Turks' was a deliberate attempt at recontextualising the crime he was about to commit, to move it back several centuries, to transfer it, into the domain of the mythical, medieval, irrational, and even fictional.

Other footage his TV crew captured, showing images of thousands of frightened people, mostly women and children but also more than two thousand men and teenage boys, crowded into the UN base in Potočari, while surrounded by heavily-armed Serb soldiers, have become well-known images of the Srebrenica genocide. These moving pictures served the purpose of eternalising 'Mladić's great Serb victory against the Turks', as Mladić repeatedly called the onslaught against Bosniak civilians.[35] The pictures also show the UN troops merely standing by while the Serb soldiers were separating men and boys from women and children. In one of the video clips available on YouTube one can see Mladić reassuring the scared people that they would be safe and even handing over chocolates to some confused children.[36] All of this was carefully staged propaganda, part of the greater, genocidal plan.[37] In the hours and days that followed all the men and boys from Srebrenica that Mladić's troops captured — 8372 of them — were killed by their captors.[38]

Mladić prepared everything in advance: all the human and material resources needed for such a large slaughter to be accomplished. The meticulous plan included eight thousand blindfolds, the same number of pieces of wire to tie the victims' hands, hundreds of thousands of bullets, some hundred buses, dozens of bulldozers, several empty stadiums, and some two thousand fit and willing executioners. It took five days to kill 8372 people; the executioners worked overtime to get 'the job' done. It was a physically exhausting exercise for those ending the lives of so many people; their fingers ached from pressing the triggers of their Kalashnikovs. Dražen Erdemović, one of those who 'worked' double shifts on these five hot July days, participating in the killings of twenty busloads of people from Srebrenica, testified later at The Hague Tribunal, 'I couldn't shoot anymore, my index finger started to go numb from

---

35 ICTY 2017.
36 See shiomiga1djura 2011.
37 Nuhanović 2007; Halilovich 2013; Bećirević 2014.
38 ICTY 2017; Halilovich 2016.

so much killing. I was killing them for hours'.[39] This is how my hometown was killed in July 1995. Spread across the first page of my Australian passport, S-R-E-B-R-E-N-I-C-A almost reads like my name and, like my name, it travels with me wherever I go. Since July 1995, my place of birth has become an even more important mark of identity — more a scar than a mark — with which I strongly identify and am identified with.

Upon learning where I come from, I know what kind of questions to expect from people: How did you survive? How many family members did you lose? Although I was not there during the 1992–95 war, the events that took place in Srebrenica at the time have had a profound and irreparable impact on my life, and even more so on the lives of my relatives and friends who remained in the 'UN Safe Area'.

More than one hundred of them remain there forever, massacred in the 1995 Srebrenica genocide, their bones mixed in mass graves spread across the green valley along the River Drina. The place of my birth has become a synonym for death and the first act of genocide on European soil since World War II, in which more than eight thousand mostly men and boys — each of whom could have been me — were rounded up and then systematically gunned down at the killing fields and warehouses prepared in advance for this purpose.

The victims shot were Bosniak men and boys, civilians from Srebrenica and the surrounding towns and villages in eastern Bosnia along the border with Serbia. Among them were often members of three generations from the same family, hundreds of fathers, sons, brothers, and cousins holding each other's hands as the only comfort, the only thing they could do for each other in these last moments. To make the killings of so many defenceless people easier to accomplish, the executioners referred to their victims as 'Turks'. But those lined up in front of the execution squads spoke the same language and shared a similar way of life to those aiming their guns at them. Among those counting their last seconds underneath the blue skies were also many who came from 'mixed families', including a significant number of those 'mixed' with Serbs. Some of the 'mixed ones' were my relatives. The killers were soldiers of the Army of Republika Srpska and special police units of the Republic of Serbia. In charge of all the forces and directly overseeing the massacres was General Ratko Mladić.

39 Drakulić 2003.

Shortly after the Srebrenica genocide and a series of following massacres in eastern Bosnia, the US-led peace initiative brokered a peace deal in Bosnia which became known as the Dayton Peace Accords (DPA). As the result of this deal, the end of the war was declared in December of 1995. Mladić's business was finished. However, the overwhelming evidence of his crimes, comprising hundreds of mass graves across Bosnia, called for an investigation and prosecution. Like Dracula and many other monster characters, Mladić made himself invisible; he disappeared into thin air as it were, that is, the thick Balkan forests or underground bunkers. There was much speculation about his disappearance. His hiding lasted sixteen long years.

As in the case of Radovan Karadžić, another prominent monster of the Bosnian war arrested in Belgrade in July 2008, Ratko Mladić's sixteen years 'on the run' were only possible with the active assistance of Serbia's state apparatus. Mladić's disappearance was never complete. At various times, he was 'sighted' at public events such as soccer matches in the heart of Belgrade, visiting restaurants, or, as a number of released videos have shown, celebrating festive occasions with family and friends. Serbian authorities must have known every detail of Mladić's movements before, during, and after July 1995. Serbia not only 'created', decorated, and protected Mladić, but also contracted him to do the job on its behalf. Thus, it was completely logical that, after his arrest, one of the first demands Ratko Mladić made to the Serbian government was to ask for his unpaid military pension, frozen a few years earlier.

He fulfilled his part of the contract and accomplished the task he was entrusted with; through 'ethnic cleansing' and genocide, he created 'Republika Srpska', the exclusive 'Lebensraum' for Serbs in Bosnia, Serbia's protégé west of the River Drina. Thus, while he zealously implemented Serbia's plan for the destruction of Bosnia, it should not be forgotten that General Ratko Mladić never waged a private war, nor ordered killings only because he enjoyed the physical and psycho-social effects of his weapons on those he targeted. That said, he can rightfully claim the copyright for a psychological warfare strategy called 'razvlačenje pameti' (stretching sanity to the breaking point) which he invented and tested in Bosnia. He regularly — and personally — insisted on this aspect of warfare being observed when targeting civilians in the cities and villages across Bosnia.

Mladić's war effort in Bosnia enjoyed wide popular support in Serbia and Montenegro (and beyond, e.g., in Russia and Greece) and was officially — and regularly — blessed by the clergy of the Serb Orthodox Church. Much of this sentiment within the Serb Orthodox Church has not changed up to this day.

Despite the heavy involvement of the Serb Orthodox Church in providing 'spiritual guidance' and moral justification for the crimes Mladić was in charge of, the 1992–95 war in Bosnia cannot be reduced simply to a religious, civil, or ethnic conflict, some 'clash of cultures' or a vampires' ball. It was rather a clash of two diametrically opposed world views and two sets of values: the exclusive Serb clerico-fascism vs the inclusive Bosnian multiculturalism.

Humanising the Monster

With a few notable exceptions, much of the 'wider context' and the 'nature' of the war in which Ratko Mladić played a key role was not mentioned in the numerous reports published after his arrest. Following the breaking news about Mladić's arrest, the media abruptly turned this story into sensationalism in the fashion of contemporary 'reality shows', reporting on trivial details such as how Mladić demanded strawberries, how he made 'jokes' about the physical looks of one of the judges who interviewed him, or how he expressed his admiration for one of the Serbian turbo-folk singers, and other such banalities. In other reports, Mladić was portrayed as a tragic father and grandfather. They were effectively humanising the monster as if they were disappointed that Mladić indeed was an old man and not a Dracula-like figure.

Media commentators then turned to speculation about his physical and psychological health and if he was fit to stand trial: among other health conditions, his sanity was questioned and it was reported that he suffered from incontinence. True, his performance at his first hearing at The Hague Tribunal was quite pitiful and showed a spent man who might have chosen insanity over accepting responsibility for the most gruesome crimes humans can inflict on fellow humans. Despite the spotlight being put on Mladić, whose crimes are well known, our attention should not be diverted from those celebrating and continuing his legacy by other means, ranging from violent demonstrations, to hate speech, to openly denying genocide and other crimes committed by those we call monsters.

Mladić made an important contribution to the persistence of the old narratives and phantasies about the Balkans. Since the wars of the 1990s, the negative images about the region prompted different states of the former Yugoslav federation to redefine themselves as being geographically, culturally, and politically outside of the Balkans. Joining the European Union has been seen as the best way to 'debalkanise', as Romania, Bulgaria, Slovenia, and Croatia have done in recent times. A more palatable term for the region has become Southeast Europe, while the term 'Western Balkans' was coined to point the direction the rest of the region — comprising Bosnia, Serbia, Montenegro, Macedonia, Kosovo, and Albania — should take, with 'Western' being associated with the progressive, civilised, and European. (Un)surprisingly, the concepts or geopolitical entities such as Eastern, Northern, and Southern Balkans have not emerged thus far.

While the political processes relating to the Balkans' EU and NATO accession have affected the discourse and metaphors about the region, the popular imagination still negotiates the fine line between monstrosity and heroism. Rather than completely eschewing one or the other, these figures function as both types of trope, superheroes and monsters, depending on whose narrative they belong to. In the case of Mladić, despite being sentenced to life imprisonment by The Hague Tribunal[40] for orchestrating genocide and crimes against humanity and his conscious promotion of 'ancient ethnic hatreds' as part of his military strategies, he remains a superhero in the Serbian imaginary. Considering this, any attempts to change the perception of the Balkans can only be completed once leaders such as Mladić are stripped of their supernatural or monstrous qualities that it is so easy to imbue them with (as this chapter itself demonstrates), and accepted for what they really are in historical terms — i.e., callous war criminals — by both the justice system and those who see them as heroes or irrational villains.

40 ICTY.

VIII
Pokémon Reaping

JULIAN STANDS ON THE TRAM IN MELBOURNE AND MY LEFT ARM REACHES up to hold the handle above me. I peer from under my raised elbow at the phone of a seated woman who is attempting to catch a Pokémon. Through her phone's screen, reality is overlaid with cartoonish graphics including an adorable Pokémon doing nothing to evade capture. She flicks a red and white sphere towards the creature and misses twice before catching it.

Pokémon Go, as you probably know, is a virtual reality game in which you travel in real space with your phone and find virtual Pokémon. Pokémon, derived from 'pocket monsters', are small and cute beasties that 'borrow on what has been a long tradition in Japan of otherworldly beings — monsters, ghosts, demons, spirits'.[1] They are as strange and diverse as the monsters on the television series Doctor Who. However, unlike the monsters on Doctor Who, Pokémon are not threatening. Instead, we are drawn to the Pokémon and we seek them to possess them. Once located, you can, as the woman on the tram was doing, 'catch' Pokémon by holding your phone up and flicking a virtual red and white ball — a Pokéball — towards it. The ensnared little creature is then 'yours'. Nintendo, the creators of Pokémon, exhorts us to 'collect them all'. There are hundreds of different kinds.

The game Pokémon Go, which was launched in 2016, has been a global triumph for Nintendo. At its peak there were twenty-seven million downloads *in a day* and a daily profit of US$16 million.[2] Many of the millions of

1 Allison 2002.
2 Humphery-Jenner 2016.

downloaders around the world travelled and traipsed in search of as-yet unacquired Pokémon. Some people have been so monomaniacal in their quest as to have caused car accidents and the deaths of others.[3] Pokémon Go has also caused national security concerns. In Indonesia, police have been banned from playing Pokémon Go owing to the distraction it causes,[4] whilst a Frenchman in Indonesia trespassed on to a military base in pursuit of Pokémon.[5]

Seeing people mediate their interactions with the world with their phones and the Pokémon Go app can be disconcerting for the unacquainted. The neuroscientist Baroness Susan Greenfield has published her deeper concerns about the impacts of ubiquitous screen technologies such as mobile phones on people's brain and their development.[6] She contrasts the way that contemporary young people spend time with screens and phone-based games with the way that she and her interviewer, author Will Self, would have spent time as children, making up games, plots, and stories.

> Now what is exciting about that time is *you* have decided to climb the tree, it hasn't asked you to climb it, the drawing pad hasn't asked you to draw on it. The making up of the game, if you and I were kids playing cowboys and Indians, we'd say 'and *then* you're going to be ambushed, and *then* I'm gonna do this and that.' Now that plot, that narrative, which is in a sense a little mini-life, it's coming from inside you [...] It's not imposed by a second-hand web-designer. It's coming from you.[7]

Greenfield has been accused of over-egging her criticisms and concerns about screen-mediated technology.[8] And indeed, I know of families who have used the hunting of Pokémon using Pokémon Go as a frame for fun and cooperative outdoor explorations. Margaret McCartney, writing in the *British Medical Journal*, weighs in on the question of 'is Pokémon Go good or bad for you?' While noting that Pokémon Go players have had to be rescued from the sea

3   Ryall 2016; AAP 2016.
4   ABC 2016.
5   AP 2016.
6   Greenfield 2015.
7   In Self 2016.
8   E.g., Robbins 2014.

and caves, McCartney accentuates the positives. Pokémon Go has enabled her to connect with people, with 'all manner of folk I wouldn't have talked to otherwise'.[9] She concludes that whereas health-promoting mobile phone apps target people who are looking to get healthy, Pokémon Go encourages walking amongst all players. 'The possibilities for apps to make the streets an active, reclaimed playground in which to have interconnected fun are boundless. Increased physical activity is a tantalising side effect'.[10]

The previous incarnations of Pokémon games began in the mid-1990s and were based around the collecting and trading of cards, board games, and games for Gameboy — a handheld game-playing device. These too have also been regarded as promoters of development and pro-social behaviour amongst children. Anne Allison describes parents of two children that she knows who believed that Pokémon 'stimulated their kids' reading, motivated them to study and learn a minutiae of facts, helped create a cooperative play atmosphere between the two children, encouraged creativity and strategy building, and fed interest in something they approach as active rather than passive consumers'.[11]

As with Pokémon Go, these previous iterations of Pokémon provoked the question 'but is it *good* for children?' David Buckingham and Julian Sefton-Green respond by acknowledging that the intellectual challenges in playing the games well are educative. Pokémon could also be said to promote 'a "common culture" among children' that crosses age, gender, and cultural differences, thus developing 'social and communicative competencies — skills in negotiation, self-confidence and even tolerance for others'.[12] Buckingham and Sefton-Green go on to caution, however, that negotiations, such as those around the trading of Pokémon collector cards, can reinforce power-differences, such as when older children bully and deceive younger ones.[13]

However, a core concern for Buckingham and Sefton-Green revolves around the economic exploitation of children (who are the focus of their article). In card collecting, 'large amounts of cash [changes] hands in the attempt to accumulate "rare" cards. "Rarity" in this case is of course a

9   McCartney 2016, 1.
10 Ibid., 1; see also LeBlanc and Chaput 2016.
11 Allison 2003, 394.
12 Buckingham and Sefton-Green 2003, 390–93.
13 Ibid., 392.

phenomenon that is artificially created by the trading card companies'.[14] The strategies undertaken to acquire rare cards — buying special 'booster packs' — has been described as 'effectively a form of gambling, as children invest in more and more "booster packs" in the (unrealistic) hope of finding their sought-after card'.[15]

Unlike board games and card trading, however, Pokémon Go does not require interaction with other people, and thus Pokémon Go manifests different kinds of concerns. Screen-based play and face-to-face interactive play have an array of substantial differences. As noted by Greenfield, first is that the rules of behaviour in the former are unilaterally decided-upon by the game-makers. Although a person's 'culture' into which they are born might be argued as presenting people with prescribed rules of behaviour, 'culture' can also accommodate interactive, spontaneous, and potentially long-lasting changes to those rules.[16] Second, screen-mediated applications are designed to induce behaviours whose fundamental purpose lies not in the benefit of the people doing the activity, but in something entirely extrinsic to those behaviours. Whereas the purpose of playing cowboys and Indians is the enjoyment, exercise, and fostering of friendships of the children playing it, the behaviours around Pokémon Go are of course aimed at the financial profit of the makers of and investors in the mobile phone application. Buckingham and Sefton-Green's comments from 2003 on this point are equally applicable to Pokémon Go.

> Pokémon is something you *do*, not just something you read or watch or 'consume'. Yet while that 'doing' clearly requires active participation on the part of the 'doers', the terms on which it is performed are predominantly dictated by forces or structures beyond their control. The practice of collecting the cards, or playing the computer game, is to a large extent determined by the work of their designers — and indeed by the operations of the market, which makes these commodities available in particular ways in the first place. The rules that govern these particular cultural practices are therefore not, by and large, open to negotiation or change.[17]

14 Ibid.

15 Ibid.

16 E.g., Lewis 1996; Seldon and Lee 2016.

17 Buckingham and Sefton-Green 2003, 379–80; emphases original.

It is worth dwelling then on how an app, which is free to download, can raise such enormous profits. Kurt Iveson outlines this and urges caution in our embrace of 'free play'.[18] Although the most evident way that Pokémon Go generates profit is though 'in-app purchases' — such as Pokécoins, which can be then used to buy things like Pokéballs — this is not the most profitable or the most concerning. A further way Niantic — Pokémon Go's creating company — can monetise their game is through companies, such as McDonald's, paying to have desirable game locations at their businesses. Thus, Pokémon Go can become a means by which retailers 'drive business' to their doors.

Most concerning for Iveson is the profit that lies in the data gathered by the Pokémon Go app from your phone and your movements. When installing Pokémon Go, you consent to the app being able to access otherwise private and irrelevant-to-the-game information, including social media profiles and contacts, which could be sold to third parties. But aggregated data about the spatial movements of players is also valuable. Of interest are 'how far they [players] are prepared to travel as part of game play; about the kinds of places they stop during game play; about the groups they travel with; and the connections they make during game play, and much more. The commercial potential of such information is huge'.[19] Thus, Iveson observes that

> even gamers who never spend a cent on in-app purchases or promotions are effectively producing information that becomes a commodity owned by Niantic. The free distribution of Pokémon Go can be likened to the free distribution of a tool that lets us make stuff that then belongs to someone else. This tool is pretty fun to use. But this should not distract us completely from what's at stake. Work might be fun but that doesn't make it any less a form of labour. And as our everyday urban lives are increasingly commodified, it's time to start seeking answers about how the spoils of our labour (or 'playbour') are collected and distributed.[20]

If it is free, as they say, then you are the product.

Anne Allison notes with respect to the Pokémania craze between 1998 and 2002, that the cute and adorable Pokémon 'soothe and comfort consumers all

18 Iveson 2016.
19 Ibid.
20 Ibid.; see also Fuchs 2014, 97–123.

the while they generate huge profits in the form they also, and promiscuously, assume as commodities'.[21] Even when Pokémon give themselves willingly to their captors, as sometimes happens as a gesture of thanks in the story-lines of Pokémon cartoons, we are still inducted into contemporary capitalism's logic. Allison notes that such wilful surrender

> is a gentler method of acquisition than attacking wild monsters with balls or winning them in battle after they have been whiplashed, pummelled, or stung. It also reimagines the bond(age) formed by freely entering into a system that will reduce them to balls. Here the representation mimics that of capitalist ideology: people who are 'free' laborers willingly contract work for a wage in an economic system built on exploitation and reification.[22]

Pokémon Go, as a recent exemplary global financial success story, gives us further insights into the nature, and some of the dissatisfactions, of contemporary capitalism. Timothy B. Lee outlines three ways in which, as per his article's title, 'Pokémon Go Is Everything That Is Wrong with Late Capitalism'. First is that as a form of entertainment, Pokémon Go does not contribute significantly to local economies, as going to a bowling alley might have done in the past. Rather than promoting local job-creation, any money spent 'goes into the pockets of the huge California- and Japan-based global companies that created *Pokémon Go*'.[23] Second, Pokémon Go exemplifies the ways in which money flows out of smaller cities and less populated regions towards big cities that are home to large digital technology companies. Thus, 'cities on the receiving end of *Pokémon Go*-style money gushers are booming so much that acute housing shortages are causing rents to skyrocket. The rest of the country [the US] has seen barely seen an economic recovery at all'. And third, whereas new industries in the twentieth century required considerable capital (such as to build factories and movie theatres), 'the *Pokémon Go* economy' — as Lee refers to it — 'is different'. This is because 'the sums [of money] involved here are tiny compared with the cost of building a new

---

21 Allison 2002.
22 Allison 2006, 230.
23 Lee 2016.

car assembly line. And Pokémon Go seems unlikely to produce very many opportunities for complementary local businesses'.[24]

The profit motive required of companies means that capital flows towards those which offer better value and higher returns, irrespective of the impact that these changes in flow have on people's live(lihood)s. This point is dramatised in the 2017 episode of Doctor Who titled 'Oxygen'. As noted before, unlike Pokémon, Doctor Who's monsters are not cute; they threaten and terrify.[25] In this episode, set on a spaceship, the Doctor, his companions, and remaining ship's crew are pursued by autonomously-functioning space suits that carry their now-dead human inhabitants inside them. We discover that these suits are not in fact haunted but are carrying out a command now programmed into them by the company that owns the ship. That command is to 'deactivate' the suits' 'organic component' because the human crew on board were no longer as profitable a workforce as the one being sent to replace them. This replacement crew is traveling on what the remaining crew members — Ivan and Abby — think is a vessel sent to rescue them after they had initiated a distress call when they thought the suits were hacked or began to malfunction.

> Abby: There's rescue ships on the way.
> Doctor: No, there isn't! No, there isn't. There never was a rescue ship.
> Ivan: What are you talking about?
> Doctor: There was no hacking, no malfunction. The suits are doing exactly what they were designed to do. What your employers are telling them to do.
> Ivan: And what would that be?
> Doctor: Save the oxygen that you are wasting. You've become inefficient. You even told me...
> Abbey: So everyone had to die?
> Doctor: Ah ha! Well, you are just organic components, and you're no longer efficient. So you're being thrown away. You don't believe me? Check on that rescue ship. Access the log.
> Abbey: No, not true. None of it. [Ivan checks the computer.] You, you are just a lunatic.
> Ivan: It is true, Abby. The ship, it set off before the distress call.

24 Ibid., 2016.
25 Cf. Orthia 2010.

Doctor: They're not your rescuers. They're your replacements. The end point of capitalism. A bottom line where human life has no value at all. We're fighting an algorithm, a spreadsheet. Like every worker, everywhere, we're fighting the suits.

The Doctor's final reference to 'the suits' is not to the space suits breaking through the doors as he speaks. 'The suits' are of course the profit-seeking, number crunching, suit-wearing company-owners whose fiduciary concern before all others is maximal profit. Just as the livelihoods of workers are secondary concerns (if that) of the profit-maximising disciples of the spreadsheet, likewise are the very lives of the workers on the spaceship. In this episode of Doctor Who, murderous space suits are not the monsters; it is capitalism that is the monster.

Is it too absurd to suggest that the quest for profit-maximisation would really lead maximisers to forfeit people's lives? Hardly. These words are being typed whilst people still remain appalled by the meagre savings made by choosing inferior cladding on Grenfell Tower, which combusted spectacularly and horrifically in June 2017, killing dozens of the building's inhabitants. This tower, says Will Self, which 'now stands blackened and carious, looming over the streets of Notting Hill and West London', is a symbol of a dystopic future. It is a symbol of

A future in which the lives of social housing tenants can indeed be priced. We may never know the final toll in the fire, and we don't know as yet which exercise in cost cutting and profit-maximization turned Grenfell Tower into a death trap. But if you were to divide the latter figure by the former, you'd discover how cheaply lives could have been saved. The dreadful truth is that the shiny new appearance of recladded blocks such as this should have alerted us to the reality we are already living in just such a dystopia.[26]

It is perhaps apt that Self points our attention to the 'shiny new appearance' of the old buildings. The new cladding on these buildings is intended to not only update, but to renew and improve our relationships with an unattractive structure, which now lies beneath an appealing exterior. Likewise in Pokémon, our relationships with the monsters are intended to be fond ones. Indeed, those

26 Self 2017; see also Moore 2017; Self 2011.

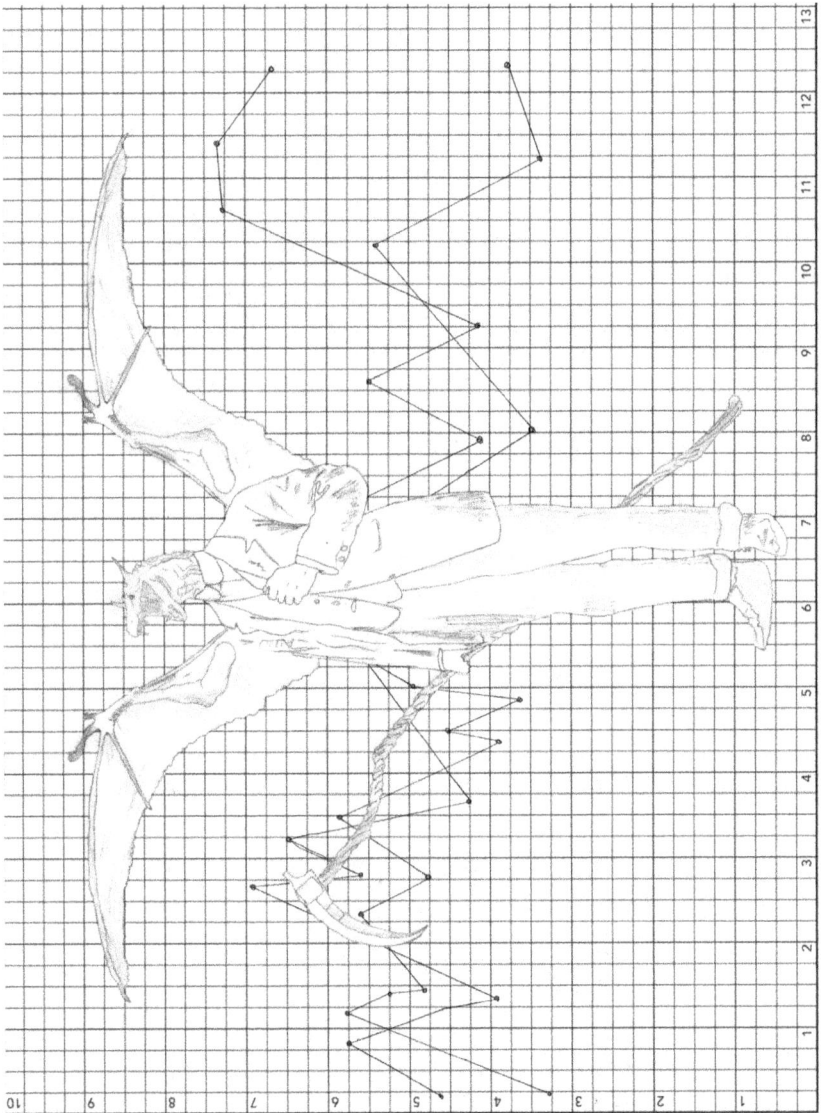

Figure 8. 'Pokémon economicus', by Al Gevers.

relationships might even be thought of as 'loving'.[27] However, the rules of the Pokémon universe require us to acquire and own them, and then to deploy, trade, or discard them at our will and at our pleasure. 'Monsters start out as wild,' writes Allison, but once trapped inside Pokéballs, they can 'be quantified and, in this respect, resemble money, which converts the qualitative difference of commodities (use values) to a quantitative equivalence (exchange value)'.[28]

Allison's critique of Pokémon appears founded in its impact on how we — especially children — are induced to view relationships under capitalism versus relationships in non-capitalist gift economies (in the sense associated with Marcel Mauss's work *The Gift*). 'Whereas in capitalism relations are used to produce things, in gift exchange things are used to produce relations'.[29]

But to what end would the various iterations of Pokémon seek to induct us into this logic? The answer is that inducting us is not the purpose of Pokémon, and any such induction is incidental. The 'core business' of Pokémon Go, for example, is the profitability of the game's owners, which is driven by us playing it and giving it our attention. In this, adorable monsters seem to have been created for our enjoyment and consumption, and we take pleasure in collecting them. However, their willingness to be reaped should disconcert us. Can it be that there are monsters that are so easily and safely domesticated? No. Whilst we wander streets and parks in a pleasurable quest to harvest Pokémon monsters, in reality it is we who are being harvested. It is the Pokémon who reap, and we who yield.

27 Allison 2006, 219.
28 Ibid., 220.
29 Ibid., 216.

IX
Godzilla, The Unmocked God

HUMANITY HAS ONLY BELATEDLY BEGUN ADDRESSING THE KNOWN AND global threat of climate change in a satisfactory way. Robert Manne notes that the consensus about the causes of climate change emerged in the 1980s, but that, 'Despite our knowledge of the harm we are inflicting, the volume of greenhouse-gas emissions that are warming the earth has increased each year since that time, recently at accelerating speed'.[1] Manne seeks to detail the array of reasons why humanity has been unable to act adequately, detailing a range of factors, from human psychological dispositions to the historical trajectory of global political affairs including the fall of communism and the ascent of neoliberalism, to the deliberate sowing of confusion by vested interests.

It is not for want of facts that we have been unable to marshal a response. And neither is it for the lack of skilful writers who can convey a sense of urgency. Naomi Klein's book *This Changes Everything: Capitalism vs. the Climate*,[2] is a compelling and accessible read that has been widely read and critically well received.[3] In it she outlines the pervasive impacts of global capitalism (to which I soon return), but also widens the concept of 'climate change denial' to include not only those who contest the reality of climate change, but also those who, like herself in earlier years, accept that it is real but who do not engage with it and pay no attention to it.[4] Her book is a thoughtful and desperate call

---

1   Manne 2015, 25.
2   Klein 2014.
3   E.g., Manne 2014.
4   Klein 2014, 3.

to action to those who remain in this form of denial. This is because 'Climate change', she affirms,

> isn't an 'issue' to add to the list of things to worry about, next to health care and taxes. It is a civilizational wake-up call. A powerful message — spoken in the language of fires, floods, droughts, and extinction — telling us that we need an entirely new economic model and a new way of sharing this planet. Telling us we need to evolve.[5]

In the conclusion of our book, we seek not to convince those uncertain of the reality of anthropogenic climate change, nor to elaborate on the array of analyses that seek to describe or account for inaction, nor to describe the many inspiring projects by diverse collectivities and organisations to promote climate action. Rather, we present an icon that may enable us to personify and dramatise the reaction of the global ecosystem to humanity's impacts upon it — impacts that some have described as potentially releasing 'climate monsters'.[6] Such reifications have been described in a number of societies, but a globally recognisable one may help us imagine more readily what sometimes seem like diffuse ecological causes and effects, to make more immediate the sometimes-delayed impacts of our actions. James Lovelock's Gaia has been one such attempt,[7] but here we describe how Godzilla, the great reptile, can also help us conceive of our impacts with an awareness of the whole of which we are a part.

The Nature of Godzilla

In drawing out the qualities of Godzilla that we believe make him apt for the role we have set for him,[8] it may be fruitful to begin by comparing Godzilla to a contemporary, Gamera. Gamera, a giant bipedal turtle, is essentially good. Although destructive in the first film in 1965, *Gamera, the Giant Monster*,

5   Klein 2014, 25.
6   E.g., Stephen Pacala in Friedman (2007); Readfern 2018.
7   Lovelock 2000.
8   Although not without some equivocation, we will refer to Godzilla as a 'him', following William Tsutsui (2004, 11–12) who argues that, although there is ambiguity, on balance the evidence favours regarding Godzilla as male.

Gamera subsequently acts as a protector of humanity against diverse threats, including aliens and other malevolent monsters. The benevolent status of Gamera is suggested in the title of the 1995 film, *Gamera: Guardian of the Universe*. He is also known as 'Friend to all children'.

Godzilla, meanwhile, is amoral. Its motivations are unknown, and Godzilla does no-one's bidding. A scene from *Godzilla in Hell* confirms this.[9] After struggling to defeat an arch-nemesis, SpaceGodzilla, Godzilla is assisted by butterfly-winged people which the reader understands to be angels. With their assistance, Godzilla reverses what seemed like impending defeat by SpaceGodzilla and the demons assisting him. The angels then command Godzilla to assist them in return. 'Now that we have aided you in your victory against SpaceGodzilla', they declare, 'you shall serve us in our battle against Hell!'

Godzilla responds by destroying the things around him and grasping a handful of angels and demons. Angels and demons alike throw their hands up in surrender and proclaim, 'We submit to you Godzilla! You are the one we worship–'. Their entreaty is concluded with Godzilla crushing them in his jaws.

Godzilla has no loyalties. Along similar lines, Tom O'Donnell observes that 'Godzilla isn't going to do what a bunch of spineless bureaucrats or corrupt lobbyists tell him to do. Godzilla goes his own way'.[10]

Writing in *The New Yorker* in 2014 after the release of Gareth Evans's Hollywood reboot of Godzilla (to which we return), Richard Brody writes that 'the creature is famous for signifying the great movie monster without actually being one'. (This is especially the case with the goofy kid-orientated ones from the 1960s, which depart considerably from the tenor of the first Godzilla film of 1954.)

Brody goes on to reflect on Godzilla as an entity and a character.

> The main problem is that Godzilla itself isn't very interesting. The monster is a principle of pure destruction: it's not feeding on human flesh or farm animals or asphalt or electricity; it's just laying waste to whatever's in its path, stomping and swatting and smashing and exhaling a fiery dragon breath for the sheer hell of it. In theory, the idea of a nihilistic monster is as good as the idea of a reflective one,

9   Stokoe et al. 2016.
10 O'Donnell 2016.

a tormented one, or a hungry one—provided that it's developed. Godzilla, the lord of the land and sea, has no objective, no goal, no guiding principle; it has been jolted from its somnolence, its habitat has been despoiled, and now it despoils ours. Godzilla is a premise, a device, and a look, but not a being; for all its violence, it's essentially static.[11]

But is Godzilla uninteresting? Surely not. Godzilla is the most franchised film series in the world — now surpassing the British comedy *Carry On* series. There are well over thirty Godzilla films. This is more than Tarzan and James Bond. Godzilla deserves our consideration.

Godzilla emerges first in 1954 in the film *Gojira*, later retitled for US release two years later as *Godzilla — King of the Monsters*. As described by Anne Allison, '*Gojira* is the story of a four-hundred-foot-tall amphibious monster awakened from his four-hundred-million-year hibernation at the bottom of the sea by nuclear testing by Americans (as they did in real life) on nearby Bikini Atoll. The blasts both enrage and mutate Gojira, turning him into a monstrous hybrid that is part dinosaur, part nuclear weapon'.[12] Allison expands on her parenthetical remark by noting that the tests were conducted in secret, but affected by the blast was the crew of twenty-three men on the Japanese trawler *Daigo Fukuyū Maru* (which translates as Lucky Dragon). Six died soon after.[13]

On the effect of Gojira for those in Japan, Allison quotes Tanaka Tomoyuki who writes that 'audiences hugely applauded Gojira. This is because in everyday life, people have to suppress their anger, and Gojira is a substitution for this. It satisfies everyone's desire for destruction'.[14] Allison goes on to observe, as is often done with Godzilla, that it 'signifies World War II as a travesty of nature brought on by the atomic blasts of the Americans'.[15] But, continues Allison, 'for Japanese audiences, then, *Gojira* provided a vehicle for reliving the terrors of the war relieved of any guilt or responsibility — solely, that is, from the perspective of victim'. But, at the same time, Gojira is empowering;

11 Brody 2014.
12 Allison 2006, 42.
13 Ibid., 45.
14 In Allison 2006, 45.
15 Ibid.

'he is scarred yet empowered by a particular historical event — a nuclear blast that disturbs his home but also rewires him as an atomic cyborg'.[16] Godzilla/Gojira dies in the 1954 film. And not for the last time. And yet, like Leviathan, Godzilla is fundamentally undefeatable. Godzilla has died, but so has God.[17] Godzilla's invincibility is important in thinking through its meaningfulness, and Godzilla's meaning in our present context is potentially profound. William Tsutsui observes that 'Godzilla has remained relevant because of his uncanny ability to reflect the shifting obsessions, anxieties, and expectations of moviegoers across decades, national boundaries, and wide cultural divides'.[18]

For Brody, 'the first "Godzilla" set its warnings against nuclear weapons and other weapons of mass destruction. In the new story [the 2014 Godzilla movie], the presumptuousness of harnessing the energy of matter is only the first in a range of other sins that add up to a misguided faith in human control over the course of nature'.[19] However, he continues with respect to Godzilla's 2014 incarnation in Gareth Edward's film, 'Edwards's "Godzilla" doesn't merely lend a biblical tone to the war of the massive beasts; it also offers a virtually religious lesson in humility'.

Personification

Humanity is today imperilled, and in diverse and complex ways. Our world's complexity — as well as its fragility — requires our attention. Everything we can observe, whether political circumstances, social phenomena, and especially environmental issues, is thoroughly complex.[20] Perhaps we should say unimaginably complex. Complexity theory and systems thinking attempt to provide an approach, a framework by which we might apprehend the phenomena around us. However, proponents of these approaches admit that there are limits to the extent that all relevant factors can be considered in a complexity-informed analysis of a given thing.[21]

---

16 Ibid., 46.
17 Nietzsche 1995.
18 Tsutsui 2014.
19 Brody 2014.
20 Boulton, Allen, and Bowman 2015.
21 Ibid., 113.

Considering everything that could or should be considered for any given problem, especially our global environmental ones, is impossible for the human mind. And confronting our minds with issues or situations that demand our attention, but which are too difficult to comprehend or face, can readily turn us away from confronting what we must. In a discussion about charitable giving in the BBC podcast series *Analysis*, it was noted that large and complex disasters provide barriers to our ability to respond usefully.

> David Edmonds: I wonder whether it is the case that if there's a small disaster with tens or hundreds [of victims], people can cope with it and are more likely to give than if there's a massive disaster which psychologically is just too big for them to be able to comprehend...
>
> Daniel Oppenheimer: Absolutely. And there's a word for that in psychology literature called 'psychophysical numbing'. We can't conceive of numbers that big. And moreover, if we can understand them, we realise that our gift will not make a big difference. It's a drop in the bucket.[22]

In their study on the ability of journalist reporting of disaster and suffering to evoke sympathetic responses from audiences, Maier et al. found in their study of 638 US based survey respondents, that 'providing factual information about a current event or issue, is often not sufficient to arouse a strong response'.[23] In fact, it evoked the weakest response of the different forms of reporting they explored. 'The reader needs to feel', they continue, 'an empathetic connection to what is happening, especially when dealing with distant large-scale suffering'.[24] Notably, they observe the significant impact that the addition of an image has on audiences.

The effect of an image can be profound and Maier et al. note the example of the global response in 2015 to the photograph of Aylan Kurdi's lifeless body on a Turkish beach.[25] Paul Barry, of Australia's television show *Media Watch*, described in September 2015 how that image had 'shocked the world, shaken

---

22 Edmonds 2016.
23 Maier et al. 2016, 14.
24 Ibid.
25 Ibid., 2–3.

politicians, and transformed the debate about refugees fleeing from war'.[26] But the potential that personification can have is not unrealised by politicians. Amid the politicisation of asylum seekers arriving by boat to Australia in the early 2000s, the Australian government, under the administration of then Prime Minister John Howard, sought to control the imagery of asylum seekers that could circulate, so that asylum seekers could not be humanised. Quoting the report from a Senate inquiry in 2002, Bleiker et al. write that 'a key reason for the ensuing tight control of photo-journalists was to "ensure that no imagery that could conceivably garner sympathy or cause misgiving about the aggressive new border protection regime would find its way into the public domain"'.[27] When people weren't as able to personify and connect with asylum seekers, their sympathies and engagement waned.

Reifying the Unmocked God

'The Unmocked God' is a chapter by Gregory Bateson in his co-authored book with Mary Catherine Bateson *Angels Fear: Towards an Epistemology of the Sacred*.[28] In it he explores three ways of understanding the world that are, in his view, more epistemologically sound than what prevailed at the time of his writing, which is little different to today. These sounder epistemologies lead us towards ways of seeing and understanding the world that are respectful of wholeness and systemic interconnectedness. In the first of the three ways, he points to the concept of '*anangke*, or necessity' in ancient Greece. The impacts of an act by someone in one generation can lead to a series of necessary and possibly unending responses through generations.

> The Greek idea of necessary sequence was, of course, not unique. What is interesting is the Greeks seem to have thought of *anangke* as a totally impersonal theme in the structure of the human world. It was as if, from the initial act onwards, dice were loaded against the participants. The theme, as it worked itself out, used human emotions and motives as its means, but the theme itself (we would vulgarly call it a 'force') was thought to be impersonal, beyond and

26 Barry 2015.
27 Bleiker et al. 2013, 412.
28 Bateson and Bateson 1979.

greater than gods and persons, a bias or warp in the structure of the universe.[29]

A similar concept that Bateson points to is perhaps more familiar to more readers: *karma*. 'The Hindu idea of *karma* is similar and differs from *anangke* only in the characteristically Hindu elaboration which includes both "good" and "bad" *karma* and carries recipes for the "burning up" of bad *karma*'.[30] Although *karma* is often spoken of as 'good' or 'bad', a more nuanced understanding of *karma* is that there is no good or bad *karma*. *Karma* is, for want of a better way of describing it, the impersonal logic inherent in existence in which every action has a reaction, every cause has an effect. The operation of *karma* is without judgment. It is without appeal or supplication, though some may seek to make amends for misdeeds, referred to colloquially as 'bad *karma*'.

A third example by Bateson comes from his time amongst the Iatmul of New Guinea. There, shamans could observe a black cloud following a person who had incurred it through wrongdoing. Such a person with black *ngglambi* would encounter misfortune. The point that Bateson draws from these examples is that '*anangke, karma*, and *ngglambi* are reified abstractions, the last being the most concretely imagined, so that shamans even "see" it'.[31]

But of what are they reified abstractions? What greater thing is condensed into *anangke, karma*, and *ngglambi*? For Bateson they are thoroughly pervasive principles or themes — regularities. He writes that he is seeking to investigate 'regularities in a system so pervasive and so determinant that we may even apply the word "god" to it'.[32] These regularities 'form a unity in which we make our home. They might be seen as the peculiarities', he writes of his apotheosis of our world, 'of a god whom we might call Eco'.[33]

Bateson then returns to the title of his chapter — 'The Unmocked God' — which is epigrammed with a biblical quote from Galatians — 'Be not deceived; God is not mocked'.

29 Bateson and Bateson 1979, 137.
30 Ibid.
31 Bateson and Bateson 1979, 138.
32 Ibid., 142.
33 Ibid.

There is a parable which says that when the ecological god looks down and sees the human species sinning against its ecology — by greed or by taking shortcuts or taking steps in the wrong order — he sighs and involuntarily sends the pollution and the radioactive fallout. It is of no avail to tell him that the offense was only a small one, that you are sorry and that you will not do it again. It is no use to make sacrifices and offer bribes. The ecological God is incorruptible and therefore is not mocked.[34]

When reading this quote, Julian recalls a comment by Richard in a context now forgotten: 'There are no externalities'. An 'externality' is a cost created by a (usually) corporate entity which it itself does not bear. Consider a factory that as a by-product creates waste, which is not safely contained and stored, but is simply released into the environment. The cost of handling this waste, which was created in the interest of the factory's owners or shareholders, is externalised, and not borne by corporation. However, within the totality of life on earth, this cost does not disappear. It is borne somewhere.

The impacts of these 'sins' as Bateson refers to them, can sometimes be difficult or slow to perceive. It took a long time to understand the impact of chlorofluorocarbons on the ozone layer, and the islands of plastic refuse floating on our oceans, such as the Great Pacific Garbage Patch,[35] are largely overlooked-by-humans. We too readily fail to observe what affects us, and to appreciate the incredible complexity of their causes. And perhaps, the scale of the complexity exceeds the capacity of human imagination. Thus Bateson posits as a god, Eco — a deified abstraction — which we might regard with reverence, so leading us to change our behaviours.

Deifying Godzilla

But if *ngglambi* is a relatively concrete reification of an abstraction, then there is also another. Just as *karma* or Eco receive no supplications and entreaties, neither does Godzilla. Godzilla is a response to our actions. In the words of Dr Serizawa referring to Godzilla, 'we may not have created this monster. But we summoned it. We brought this on ourselves'.[36] Godzilla, borne of human

---

34 Ibid.
35 Greenpeace 2014; Milman 2016; Bradley 2018; Lemanksi 2018.
36 Borenstein et al. 2014, 34.

abuse, destroyer of cities, is also a reification — a deification perhaps — of what Eco also is. Irrespective of whether he harms humanity, Godzilla responds to humanity's mistreatments, and may restore the balance, or wipe the canvas clean of us. Whether we offer our respect or not, Godzilla will take it.

Thus we posit the Godzilla Principle. It is not, as some management texts have it, that you should address problems while they are small, because 'left unchecked and uncared for, they wax, not wane, until they are too big to handle, until they're too big to solve. Thus it's best to check them when they're small'.[37] Sensible as this might be, our Godzilla Principle is starker and grimmer. The Godzilla Principle is that there is no forgiveness.

Writing more narrowly for the US context, Tom O'Donnell's admiration of Godzilla is worth noting.

> I feel like our country is on the wrong track. I feel like, when I was a kid, things were better (no bills) and that, now that I'm an adult, I'm getting screwed all the time (several bills). I feel like, if Godzilla wrecks everything, that would be good (no more bills for a while). When it comes down to it, I feel like Godzilla is strong; I feel like Godzilla is powerful; I feel like Godzilla always wins (except against King Kong that one time).[38]

Reference to the 'wrong track' and to 'bills', here, deserves exploration. What might this 'wrong track' be? Gregory Bateson tells us that 'Every human individual — every organism — has his or her personal habits of how he or she builds knowledge, and every cultural, religious, or scientific system promotes particular epistemological habits'.[39] As this is the case, Bateson asks, 'Is it possible to be Epistemologically *wrong*? Wrong at the very root of thought?'[40] Yes, he concludes; in fact, 'to be wrong in Epistemology could be lethal'.[41]

Recall that Bateson's book *Angels Fear* is subtitled *Towards an Epistemology of the Sacred*, and within that title is as direct a suggestion as we receive from Gregory Bateson as to what a non-wrong epistemology would value — the sacredness of the wholeness that comes to be reified or deified as Eco. A

37 Bradbury and Garrett 2005, 140.
38 O'Donnell 2014.
39 Bateson and Bateson 1979, 20.
40 Ibid., 23.
41 Ibid., 24.

clearer understanding of the nature of a wrong epistemology is provided by Roy A. Rappaport, whose works lean heavily on Gregory Bateson's. Speaking of ways of understanding the world — epistemologies — Rappaport points out that the specialisation of academic fields undermines our ability to see things holistically. 'Facts breed facts, and as knowledge of facts burgeons the domains into which they are organized are severed into yet smaller pieces, as individuals and their knowledge become increasingly specialized. The result is the loss of the sense of the world's wholeness'.[42] Rappaport goes on to say that 'In the realm of fact nothing is sacred except, perhaps, the maxim "nothing is sacred," and knowledge that had been ultimately sacred is no longer knowledge at all. It is "mere belief"'.[43]

Michael D. Jackson's recollection of an incident he observed whilst conducting fieldwork with the Walpiri in Australia's Northern Territory will help me to draw out the point I, Julian, am moving towards. He observed the existential angst that followed when a sacred tree was destroyed when it was used as an anchor to winch out a bogged vehicle being driven by white mining-company employees. The damaging of a sacred tree, which was not only 'the loss of the tree but the loss of a link to the past' — to its custodians' Dreaming. 'I'm sad now', said Clancy, one such custodian, to Jackson. 'I can't show my children that tree. My father told me that Dreaming [...] but I can't show it to my son'.[44]

The damage could not be allowed to go without retribution, but the form of that retribution towards the white occupants of that vehicle is revealing. 'We got to hurt those whitefellas', said Clancy, 'so they're more careful in future. We got to make them pay'.[45] Jackson describes the form of the retribution:

> In the opinion of many Walpiri, the thing most precious to whites, more dear than life, was money. To hit them where it hurt, one would have to exact financial retribution. 'We say money is the whitefella Dreaming', Clancy said.[46]

---

42 Rappaport 1999, 450; see also Kingsnorth 2017, 153–79.

43 Ibid., 450.

44 Jackson 1995, 139.

45 Ibid., 140.

46 Ibid., 140.

Describing money as the Dreaming of 'whitefellas' imbues the now globalised imperative towards financial gain with the religious air it deserves. '[E]conomic rationality', Rappaport writes, 'is not only given free rein but is even elevated to the status of general organizing principle and may even claim sanctity'.[47] Thus when O'Donnell highlights 'bills' as his bane, we can read this bane more generally as that of the financial imperative that has been placed at the heart of the global order, with all other values subjected to its primacy.[48]

And when O'Donnell refers to 'my country' as being on the wrong track, it is perhaps no accident that he writes from the US, for Rappaport cites a maxim that exemplifies this misguided epistemology: 'The Business of America is Business'.[49] One fragment of humankind's travails is now elevated to the whole in the form of '*Homo economicus*' — economic man — whose intelligence and being is not orientated towards acting with 'wisdom' as *Homo sapiens* should act — but acting with a view to extracting maximum economic value. '*Homo economicus* becomes the *moral* as well as natural model of humanity'.[50] The almighty dollar has made humanity monstrous. '*Homo economicus*', according to Rappaport, is 'that golem of the economists into which life has been breathed not by the persuasiveness of their theory but by its coerciveness'.[51]

While the nature of contemporary capitalism was explored in the previous chapter through sweet collectible Pokémon, we here see the profound impacts of that 'monetary epistemology'[52] which has created golem out of humanity and will bring to pass global systemic change, one way or the other. Naomi Klein, speaking about the crux of her book *This Changes Everything*, says that

> we find ourselves in this moment where there are no non-radical options left before us. Change or be changed, right? And what we mean by that is that climate change, if we don't change course, if we don't change our political and economic system, is going to change everything about our physical world. And that is what climate scientists are telling us when they say business as usual leads to three to four degrees Celsius of warming. That's the road we are on.

47 Rappaport 1999, 450; see also 460.
48 See also Battersby 2014, 129, 145.
49 Rappaport 1999, 450–51.
50 Ibid., 451; emphasis added.
51 Ibid., 461.
52 Ibid., 460.

We can get off that road, but we're now so far along it, we've put off the crucial policies for so long, that now we can't do it gradually. We have to swerve, right? And swerving requires such a radical departure from the kind of political and economic system we have right now that we pretty much have to change everything.[53]

To perhaps overcome the overwhelmingness of our present circumstances, an abstraction may be helpful to inspire the urgency, and especially the awe, required to disturb us from complacency, to help us to appreciate our fragility. No other monster is as well placed to do this for the world as Godzilla. Our imagination of Godzilla and its size tracks our own skyscraping towers — as they have grown in height, so has Godzilla — keeping apace with our conception of enormity.

Mass is not Godzilla's only awe-inspiring trait, for if it was, Gamera, the good turtle, could also play this role, being as large or larger than Godzilla. But Gamera cannot play this role. It works to protect the human status quo, which Klein tells us is disturbed.

That Godzilla has in the past been portrayed as the active saviour of mankind is something we can set aside. Godzilla, especially in the films of the 1960s, vanquished mankind's threats, and so we could consider Godzilla no different to Gamera. But Godzilla began in 1954 as an amoral creature and he has returned to amorality in the 2010s. The Japanese film *Shin Godzilla* of 2016 is such an instance of this rendering; it is a reboot of the original 1954 story, told, however, with different backdrops, including the 2011 Triple Disaster in Fukushima prefecture. It is worth noting that *Shin* here was deliberately chosen to accommodate multiple meanings. 'While it can be translated as "New Godzilla," it can also mean "True Godzilla," and "God Godzilla"'.[54]

You might think that asking Godzilla to play this deified role is too much. Godzilla has for most of his life been played by a man in a Godzilla-suit, and with B-grade special effects. However, although this has been the case, Godzilla does bring ourselves into perspective. Our buildings succumb to it. Towers taking years to erect are razed in moments. And they are brought down either as a response to humanity's doings, or perhaps even more frighteningly, incidentally. To Godzilla, we are marginalia. Anthony Lane captures the potential of Godzilla. Referring to moments in the 2014 Hollywood version

53 Klein quoted in Winship 2016.
54 ANN 2016.

of Godzilla in which Godzilla battles his monster foes, Lane writes 'by now, the beasts are barely distinguishable: an abstract, infernal chaos of warty skin and swipes of vicious claw. That's what the perfect "Godzilla" should be: no character development, no backstory, no winsome kids, just hints and glimpses of immeasurable power'.[55]

In the 2014 iteration, Godzilla's behaviour does in fact rescue humanity by exterminating his giant adversaries, MUTO — Massive Unidentified Terrestrial Objects — which feed on nuclear energy. But as academic and Godzilla fan William Tsutsui observes, 'any urge to defend humankind is an accidental byproduct of the instincts he developed to survive in some distant primordial ecosystem'.[56] Godzilla pursues the MUTO because being at 'the top of the prehistoric food chain, the monster is compelled to hunt down and kill his ancient parasitic prey'.[57] But the fact that Godzilla might sometimes and incidentally work to the benefit of humanity is not out of line with the workings of that which Godzilla represents. Segments of humanity have occasionally caught some lucky breaks.[58] But whether as beneficiaries or otherwise, the point remains that, as delivered by Dr Serizawa in the form of cliché, but a cliché still mostly unheeded: 'the arrogance of man is thinking that nature is under our control, and not the other way around'.

We know that in the above we are seeking to imbue Godzilla with a particular interpretation, but one that is supported by its representations and reflected in common construals. This interpretation presents Godzilla as a global icon with which we can apprehend the perils of our planetary and ecosystemic impacts. Godzilla is, then, both a monster of our modernity, and a monster for our modernity.

55 Lane 2014.
56 Tsutsui 2014.
57 Ibid.
58 E.g., Ravilious 2017; Clark, 2012; Wild, 2012.

Figure 9. Image from the film Shin Godzilla.

Authorship, Acknowledgements, and Other Notes Not Elsewhere Well-Accommodated

WHEN THE AUTHORS OF THIS BOOK FIRST MET TO DISCUSS HOW MONSTERS could be used to explore our contemporary global condition, we also deliberated on some aspects of the style and presentation of the text. Of the latter, we affirmed that our writing would be, at least occasionally, in the first person. A challenge that a multi-authored book poses to first-person writing is that when 'I' is used, it is unclear which of the five authors wrote the sentence that featured the 'I'. However, as this book was being conceived, Julian also observed his daughter and son who were in their early months of speaking. I observed at that time that they would refer to themselves in the third person. I came to think of this mode of speaking of oneself in the third person, which among adults is common in some languages, as the Third Person Personal. In the context of this book, this evolved into the convention that the author of a given chapter would, in the first instance of first-person writing, refer to him- or herself in the third person by name, and thereafter with 'I'.

With this convention in mind, the reader will be able to know which of this book's five co-authors was the primary composer of a given chapter. We do not, however, label each chapter as *by* a certain author because this would fail to convey the way our cooperation, consideration, discussion *et cetera* formed an ether in which the chapters came into being. Although we each took our own approach, and although each chapter retains the tone and character of the writing of its author, the other co-authors were not absent. They were presences, presences that sometimes materialised in person in corridors and office doors to chat about monsters. At other times though, co-authors haunted each other, sometimes in the form of the values and perspectives that a given author represented for another.

There are some conventions to which this book has intentionally not conformed. One of those is the already noted conception of authorship. Another lies in the absence of an 'Introduction'. Introductions, as I have noted to my co-authors, are chapters that I have always experienced negatively. I experience introductions as things to be suffered through before one actually got started with the text proper. For supporting our intentional omission of an introduction, this book's other unconventional features, and the book in general, we are grateful to our anonymous reviewers, whose suggestions and critical appraisal of the chapters were all gratefully received, and almost all of which were acted upon.

The absence of an introduction in this book is admittedly more personal than ideological. What is ideological, however, is our choice of publisher. There are countless published critiques of neoliberalism, of capitalism, and of inequalities between and within peoples and countries. Many of these critiques are published with publishers that are themselves propelled principally by financial gain and which publish their books with a view, primarily, of making a profit for owners or shareholders. There are, of course, a number of publishers that are not-for-profit entities. However, finding one that then also made their texts globally available *and* affordable was difficult — that is, until we encountered Kısmet Press, a not-for-profit academic publisher that publishes all its texts online. We thank Kısmet Press, in particular our corresponding editor Dr Tim Barnwell, for their interest in and efforts with our book.

Kısmet Press is guided by an ethos (which can be viewed on their website) that affirms the public good that comes from making their publications readable in their entirety online for free. However, books and e-books can also be purchased, and it is through these purchases that Kısmet Press' not-for-profit operations are sustained. For those who can afford it, we would encourage those readers to purchase a book from Kısmet Press (whether the present book in hardcopy or another), to support its work. In the case of *Monsters of Modernity*, however, we have made it free to download. This was achieved by the authors waiving their royalties and through funding kindly provided by the School of Global, Urban and Social Studies at RMIT, with which the authors have (or at one time had) an association.

The authors take this moment to acknowledge the people of the Woi wurrung and Boon wurrung language groups of the eastern Kulin Nations on whose unceded lands RMIT stands and on which the chapters were authored. We respectfully recognise Ancestors and Elders, past and present. Readers of our book will find that every chapter is accompanied by an image. Three of these were drawn specifically for this book by the young Australian activist and emerging artist Al Gevers. Another illustration, which accompanies Hariz's chapter on vampires and Ratko Mladić, was provided by the sculptor and artist of Bosnian heritage, Adis Elias Fejzić. The image on our book's cover is from the Broached Monsters Collection, designed by Trent Jansen for Broached Commissions, in which Australian Indigenous mythological figures — in this case the Central Australian Pankalangu — are explored and interpreted. We are grateful for being permitted to use these images which, along with others in this book, help bring some of the ideas and concepts of each chapter to greater life, and constitute another form of communication that is largely disregarded in 'scholarly' publishing for diverse reasons, including no doubt the primacy of logocentrism in academia. While the inclusion of images in a book is hardly uncommon, we share the opinion of Paul Kingsnorth who asserts that artists of all kinds have a role in challenging the destructive myth of 'civilisation',[1] which we note in Chapter 1.

Finally, and as has been noted in more than one chapter in this book, our world's biodiversity is plummeting. It is at the highest rate since the extinction of the dinosaurs. This fact is so many things: it is a tragedy, it is sad, it is alarming, it is a symptom. That of which it is a symptom is itself many things, and we have tried to reveal and address it through the monsters that feature in our book. But in recognition of this calamity, we dedicate this book to two fitting creatures whose region of the world is shared with this book's authors. We dedicate this book to the Tasmanian Devil — which is now endangered as a result of the spread of Devil Facial Tumour Disease — and to the Western Long-beaked Echidna — which shares its name with the ancient Greek 'mother of monsters'. Unlike most endangered animals, however, there is hope for both the Tasmanian Devil and the Western Long-beaked Echidna as they are the focus of efforts to protect them from extinction — efforts that should, of course, be demanded for all species at risk.

1   Kingsnorth 2017, 273.

References

AAP (2016) 'Pokémon Go Player Crashes Car into School while Playing Game'. *The Guardian* 29 July. Available at: https://www.theguardian. com/australia-news/2016/jul/29/pokemon-go-player-crashes-car-into-school-while-playing-game (accessed 12 February 2019).

ABC (2016) 'Pokemon Go: Indonesia Bans Police from Playing Game while on Duty; Warns Game Could Be Used to Spy'. *ABC News* 20 July. Available at: http://www.abc.net.au/news/2016-07-20/indonesia-bans-police-troops-from-playing-pokemon-go/7645798 (accessed 4 July 2017).

Allam, L. (2018) 'In 1788 It Was Nothing but Bush': Tony Abbott on Indigenous Australia'. *The Guardian* 29 August. Available at: https:// www.theguardian.com/australia-news/2018/aug/29/in-1788-it-was-nothing-but-bush-tony-abbott-on-indigenous-australia (accessed 29 August 2018).

Allan, T. (2008) *The Mythic Bestiary: The Illustrated Guide to the World's Most Fantastical Creatures*. London: Duncan Baird.

Allison, A. (2002) 'The Cultural Politics of Pokémon Capitalism'. Paper Presented at Medi-in-Transition 2: Globalization and Convergence Conference, Massachusetts Institute of Technology, Cambridge, MA.

Allison, A. (2003) 'Portable Monsters and Commodity Cuteness: Pokémon as Japan's New Global Power'. *Postcolonial Studies* 6(3): 381–95.

Allison, A. (2006) *Millennial Monsters: Japanese Toys and the Global Imagination*. Berkeley: University of California Press.

Allison, A. (2008) 'Pocket Capitalism and Virtual Intimacy: Pokemon as Symptom of Postindustrial Youth Culture'. In: Cole, J., and D. L., Durham (Eds.), *Figuring the Future: Globalization and the Temporalities of Children and Youth*. Santa Fe: School for Advanced Research Press: 179–95.

Allison, P. R. (2014) 'The Castle of Otranto: The Creepy Tale That Launched Gothic Fiction', *BBC News Magazine* 13 December. Available at: http://www.bbc.com/news/magazine-30313775 (accessed 2 October 2017).

Anderson, B. (2006) *Imagined Communities: Reflections on the Origin and Spread of Nationalism*. New York: Verso.

Anghie, A. (2007) *Imperialism, Sovereignty and the Making of International Law* (Vol. 37). Cambridge: Cambridge University Press.

ANN (2016) 'Shin Godzilla/Godzilla: Resurgence Film Opens in Singapore on August 25'. *AnimeNewsNetwork* 28 July. Available at: http://www.animenewsnetwork.com/news/2016-07-28/shin-godzilla-godzilla-resurgence-film-opens-in-singapore-on-august-25/.104756 (accessed 7 September 2016).

Anzulović, B. (1999) *Heavenly Serbia: From Myth to Genocide*. New York: New York University Press.

AP (2016) 'French Pokémon Go Player Arrested on Indonesian Military Base'. *The Guardian* 19 July. Available at: https://www.theguardian.com/technology/2016/jul/19/french-pokemon-go-player-arrested-on-indonesian-military-base (3 July 2017).

Arcaya, J. M. (1979) 'A Phenomenology of Fear'. *Journal of Phenomenological Psychology* 10(2): 165–88.

Arendt, H. (1973) *The Origins of Totalitarianism*. Orlando: Houghton Mifflin Harcourt.

Asma, S. T. (2009) *On Monsters: An Unnatural History of Our Worst Fears*. Oxford: Oxford University Press.

Assmann, J. (2011 [1992]) *Cultural Memory and Early Civilization: Writing, Remembrance, and Political Imagination*. Wilson, D. H. (Trans.). Cambridge: Cambridge University Press.

Backe, E. L. (2014) 'The Devil in Disguise: Modern Monsters and their Metaphors'. *The Geek Anthropologist* 11 July. Available at: https://thegeekanthropologist.com/2014/07/11/the-devil-in-disguise-modern-monsters-and-their-metaphors/ (accessed 9 July 2017).

Bailey, A. (2008) 'Monsters: Classical to Contemporary Symbols'. *Culture, Society and Praxis* 7(1): 8–12.

Bailey, K. (1986) *Human Paleopsychology: Applications to Aggression and Pathological Processes*. Mahwah, NJ: Lawrence Earlbaum Associates.

Bakic-Hayden, M. (1995) 'Nesting Orientalisms: The Case of Former Yugoslavia'. *Slavic Review* 54(4): 917–31.

Bane, T. (2016) *Encyclopedia of Beasts and Monsters in Myth, Legend and Folklore*. Jefferson, North Carolina: McFarlan & Company.

Barrett, C. (1946) *The Bunyip and Other Mythical Monsters and Legends*. Melbourne: Reed & Harris.

Barrow, M. V. (1971) 'A Brief History of Teratology to the Early 20th Century'. *Teratology* 4: 119–30.

Barry, P. (2015) 'The Power of an Image'. *Media Watch* 14 September. Available at: http://www.abc.net.au/mediawatch/transcripts/s4312433.htm (accessed 7 September 2016).

Bateson, G. and Bateson, M. C. (1979) *Angels Fear: Toward an Epistemology of the Sacred*. New York: Macmillan.

Battersby, P. (2014) *The Unlawful Society: Global Crime and Security in a Complex World*. London: PalgraveMacMillan.

Bauman, Z. (2000) *Modernity and the Holocaust*. Cornell University Press.

Bauman, Z. (2006) *Liquid Fear*. Cambridge: Polity.

Beal, T. (2002) *Religion and its Monsters*. New York: Routledge.

Beard, J. (2007) *The Political Economy of Desire: International Law, Development and the Nation State*. Abingdon: Routledge-Cavendish.

Bećirević, E. (2015) *Genocide on the River Drina*. New Haven: Yale University Press.

Beck, U. (1992) 'From Industrial Society to the Risk Society: Questions of Survival, Social Structure and Ecological Enlightenment'. *Theory, Culture and Society* 9: 97–123.

Beck, U. (2006) 'Living in the World Risk Society'. *Economy and Society* 35(3): 329–45.

Beenstock, Z. (2015) 'Lyrical Sociability: The Social Contract and Mary Shelley's Frankenstein'. *Philosophy and Literature* 39(2): 406–21.

Benjamin, W. (2004 [1996]) 'The Metaphysics of Youth' [1913–14]. Livingstone, R. (Trans.). In: Bullock, M. and Jennings, M. W. (Eds.), *Walter Benjamin: Selected Writings, Volume 1: 1913–1926*. Reprint. Cambridge, MA: Harvard University Press: 6–17.

Berger, A. (1991 [1953]) *Encyclopedic Dictionary of Roman Law. Transactions of the American Philosophical Society* N.S. 53(2): 333–808. Reprint. Philadelphia: The American Philosophical Society.

Berger, J. (1996) 'The Chauvet Cave'. *The Guardian* 16 November. London.

Besson, S. (2011) 'Sovereignty', *Oxford Public International Law*. Available at: http://opil.ouplaw.com/view/10.1093/law:epil/9780199231690/law-9780199231690-e1472 (accessed 25 April 2018).

Best, S. (1988) 'Here Be Dragons'. *The Journal of the Polynesian Society* 97(3): 239–59.

Beville, M. (2014) *The Unnameable Monster in Literature and Film*. New York: Routledge.

Bleiker, R. (2013) 'The Visual Dehumanisation of Refugees'. *Australian Journal of Political Science* 48(4): 398–416.

Bompiani, G. (1989) 'The Chimera Herself'. In: Feher, M., Naddaff, R., and Tazi, N. (Eds.), *Fragments for a History of the Human Body*, Vol. 1., New York: Zone: 365-409.

Bonneuil, C. and J.-B. Fressoz, (2017) *The Shock of The Anthropocene: The Earth, History and Us*. London: Verso.

Boose, L. E. (2002) 'Crossing the River Drina: Bosnian Rape Camps, Turkish Impalement, and Serb Cultural Memory', *Signs* 8(1): 71–96.

Borenstein, M., Borenstein, G., Battle, E., Guichet, Y. and Loughbridge, L. (2014) *Godzilla: Awakening*. Legendary Comics: Burbank.

Borges, J. L. (2002 [1970]) *The Book of Imaginary Beings*. Reprint. London: Vintage Books.

Boucher, D. (2018) *Appropriating Hobbes: Legacies in Political, Legal, and International Thought*. Oxford: Oxford University Press.

Bowman, C. (1999) 'The Story of Words: mon.ster'. *Literary Cavalcade* 52(3): 40.

Bradbury, D. and Garrett, D. (2005) *Herding Chickens: Innovative Techniques for Project Management*. San Fransisco: Harbor Light Press.

Bradley, J. (2018) 'Ocean's End: How the World's Oceans and All Marine Life Are on the Brink of Total Collapse'. *The Monthly* August: 32–43.

Bradshaw, P. (2014) 'Leviathan Review – a Compellingly Told, Stunningly Shot Drama'. *The Guardian* 7 November. Available at: https://www. theguardian.com/film/2014/nov/06/leviathan-review-story-of-job (accessed 22 April 2018).

Breen, S. (1990) 'Land and Power in the District of Deloraine: 1825–75'. *Papers and Proceedings: Tasmanian Historical Research Association* 37(1): 23–33.

Breen, S. (1991) 'The Pall-i-torre' and 'Black and White: The Struggle for the Land'. In: *Meander Valley Memories*. Meander: Meander Primary School: 1–18.

Breen, S. (2000) 'Local Authority in Colonial Tasmania 1858–1898'. *Journal of Australian Colonial History* 2(1): 29–49.

Breen, S. (2001) *Contested Places: Tasmania's Northern Districts from Ancient Times to 1900*. Hobart: Centre for Tasmanian Historical Studies.

Brody, R. (2014) 'The Secrets of Godzilla'. *The New Yorker* 18 April. Available at: http://www.newyorker.com/culture/richard-brody/the-secrets-of-godzilla (accessed 7 September 2016).

Boulton, J. G., Allen, P. M. and Bowman, C. (2015) *Embracing Complexity: Strategic Perspectives for an Age of Turbulence*. Oxford: Oxford University Press.

Buchan, B., and Heath, M. (2006) 'Savagery and Civilization: From Terra Nullius to the "Tide of History"'. *Ethnicities* 6(1): 5–26.

Buckingham, D. and Sefton-Green, J. (2003) 'Gotta catch 'em all: Structure, Agency and Pedagogy in Children's Media Culture'. *Media, Culture and Society* 25: 379–99.

Bunnell, T. (1999) 'Views from Above and Below: The Petronas Twin Towers and/in Contesting Visions of Development in Contemporary Malaysia'. *Singapore Journal of Tropical Geography* 20(1):1–23.

Bush, G. W. (2001a) 'President Bush: "No Nation Can Be Neutral in This Conflict"'. *The White House*. Available at: https://georgewbush-whitehouse.archives.gov/news/releases/2001/11/20011106-2.html (accessed 16 September 2016).

Bush, G. W. (2001b) 'President Urges Readiness and Patience'. *The White House*. Available at: https://georgewbush-whitehouse.archives.gov/news/releases/2001/09/20010915-4.html (accessed on 16 September 2016).

Buturović, A. (2015) *Carved in Stone, Etched in Memory: Death, Tombstones and Commemoration in Bosnian Islam*. Farnham: Ashgate.

Cairnie, J. (2002) 'Imperial Poverty in Robert Tressell's *The Ragged Trousered Philanthropists*'. *The Journal of Commonwealth Literature* 37(2): 175–94.

Canguilhem, G. (1962) 'Monstrosity and the Monstrous' (Trans. T. Jaeger). *Diogenes* 10(40): 27–42.

Carey, A. (2010) *The Unwritten, Vol. 1: Tommy Taylor and the Bogus Identity*. New York: Vertigo (DC Entertainment).

Cigar, N. (1995) *Genocide in Bosnia: The Policy of 'Ethnic Cleansing' in Eastern Europe*. College Station: Texas A&M University Press.

Clarke, B. (1995) *Allegories of Writing: The Subject of Metamorphosis*. Albany, NY: State University of New York Press.

Clark, D. (2012) 'What Is Global Dimming?' *The Guardian* 11 May. Available at: https://www.theguardian.com/environment/2012/may/11/global-dimming-pollution (accessed 7 September 2016).

Cobbs, J. L. (1990) 'Alien as Abortion Parable'. *Literature/ Film Quarterly* 18(3): 198–201.

Cohen, J. (1990) 'Here Be Dragons'. *Journal of Biological Education* 24(3): 158–60.

Cohen, J. J. (1996) 'Monster Culture (Seven Theses)'. In J. J. Cohen (Ed.), *Monster Theory*. Minneapolis: University of Minneapolis Press: 3-25.

Connolly, W. E. (2013) *The Fragility of Things: Self-Organising Processes, Neoliberal Fantasies, and Democratic Activism*. Durham: Duke University Press.

Coolidge, F. L. and T. Wynn (2009) *The Rise of Homo sapiens: The Evolution of Modern Thinking*. Chichester: Wiley-Blackwell.

Cooper, Q. (2013) 'Iranian Earthquake; Zebrafish; Curiosity Rover'. *Material World* 22 April. Available at: http://www.bbc.co.uk/programmes/b01rw3yh (accessed 6 September 2016).

Creative Spirits (2018) 'Walk-off at Wave Hill: Birth of Aboriginal land Rights', *Creative Spirits*. Available at: https://www.creativespirits.info/aboriginalculture/politics/aboriginal-people-strike-walk-off-at-wave-hill (accessed 26 September 2018).

Cudd, A., and Eftekhari, S. (2018) 'Contractarianism'. In: Zalta, E. N. (Ed.), *The Stanford Encyclopedia of Philosophy* (Summer 2018 Edition). Available at: https://plato.stanford.edu/archives/sum2018/entries/contractarianism/ (accessed 23 May 2018)

Dargis, M. (2014) 'Life: Poor, Nasty, Brutish and (Probably) Short'. *New York Times* 24 December. Available at: https://www.nytimes.com/2014/12/25/movies/leviathan-turns-on-a-modern-day-job.html (accessed 22 April 2018).

Darian-Smith, E. (2013) *Laws and Societies in Global Contexts: Contemporary Approaches*. Cambridge: Cambridge University Press.

Deacon, T. (1997) *The Symbolic Species: The Co-Evolution of Language and the Human Brain*. London: Penguin.

Dell, C. (2016) *Monsters: A Bestiary of the Bizarre*. Reprint. London: Thames & Hudson.

Denham, J. (2015) 'Sigourney Weaver Reveals She Hates Alien vs Predator as Much as Everyone Else'. *The Independent* 21 July. Available at: https://www.independent.co.uk/arts-entertainment/films/news/

sigourney-weaver-reveals-she-hates-alien-vs-predator-as-much-as-everyone-else-then-randomly-turns-up-10404025.html (accessed 28 October 2017).

Derrida, J. (2009) *The Beast & the Sovereign* (Bennington, G. Trans). Vol. 1. Chicago: The University of Chicago Press.

Doak, B. R. (2014) *Consider Leviathan: Narratives of Nature and the Self in Job*. Minneapolis: Fortress.

Donaldson, T. and Dunfee, T. W. (1999) *Ties That Bind: A Social Contracts Approach to Business Ethics*. Boston: Harvard Business School Press.

Donaldson, T. and Dunfee, T. W. (2002) 'Ties That Bind in Business Ethics: Social Contracts and Why They Matter'. *Journal of Banking & Finance* 26(9): 1853–65.

Donia, R. (2006) *Sarajevo: A Biography*. Ann Arbor: University of Michigan Press.

Douglas, M. (1970) 'The Healing Rite'. *Man* 5(2): 302–08.

Drakulić, S. (2003) *They Would Never Hurt a Fly*. Boston: Little, Brown & Co.

Draus, P., and Roddy, J. (2016) 'Ghosts, Devils, and the Undead City: Detroit and the Narrative of Monstrosity'. *Space and Culture* 19(1): 67–79.

Drew, E. (1995) *On the Edge: The Clinton Presidency*. New York: Touchstone.

Durkheim, E. (1995) *The Elementary Forms of Religious Life*. New York: The Free Press.

Eagleton, T. (1999) 'Allergic to Depths'. *London Review of Books* 18 March (6): 7–8.

Ehrnström-Fuentes, M., and Kröger, M. (2017) 'In the Shadows of Social Licence to Operate: Untold Investment Grievances in Latin America'. *Journal of Cleaner Production* 141: 346–58.

Elder, B. (2003) *Blood on the Wattle, Massacres and Maltreatment of Aboriginal Australians Since 1788*. Chatswood, NSW: New Holland Publishers.

Edmonds, D. (2016) 'The Charitable Impulse'. *Analysis* 3 July. Available at: http://www.bbc.co.uk/programmes/b07h6zg7 (accessed 14 February 2019).

Elahi, S. (2011) 'Here Be Dragons...Exploring the 'Unknown Unknowns'. *Futures* 43: 196–201.

Falk, P. and Martin, G. (2007) 'Misconstruing Indigenous Sovereignty: Maintaining the Fabric of Australian Law'. In: Moreton-Robinson, A. (Ed.), *Sovereign Subjects: Indigenous Sovereignty Matters*. Crows Nest, NSW: Allen & Unwin.

Fisher, M. (2016) *The Weird and the Eerie*. London: Repeater.

Fitzpatrick, P. (2002) '"No Higher Duty": Mabo and the Failure of Legal Foundation'. *Law and Critique* 13(3): 233–52.

Fitzmaurice, A. (2007) 'The Genealogy of Terra Nullius'. *Australian Historical Studies*, 38(129): 1–15.

Flyn, C. (2016) *Thicker Than Water: A Memoir of Family, Secrets, Guilt and History*. Sydney: Harper Collins.

Foresman, G. A., and Tobienne, F., Jr. (2013) 'Aristotle's Metaphysics of Monsters and Why We Love *Supernatural*'. In: G. A. Foresman (Ed.), *Supernatural and Philosophy: Metaphysics and Monsters...for Idjits*. Hoboken, NJ: John Wiley & Sons: 16–25.

Franzen, C. E. (2007) 'Revulsion and Desire: The Figure of the Monster in Roman Imperial Imagination'. PhD Dissertation, Classics Department, University of Washington.

Fraundorfer, M. (2017) 'The Role of Cities in Shaping Transnational Law in Climate Governance'. *Global Policy* 8: 23–31.

Friedman, T. L. (2007) 'The Power of Green', *New York Times* 17 April. Available at: https://www.nytimes.com/2007/04/15/magazine/15green.t.html (accessed 9 October 2018).

Freud, S. (1913) *Totem and Taboo: Resemblances between the Psychic Lives of Savages and Neurotics*. New York: Moffat, Yard and Company.

Frynas, J. G., and Stephens, S. (2015) 'Political Corporate Social Responsibility: Reviewing Theories and Setting New Agendas'. *International Journal of Management Reviews* 17(4): 483–509.

Fuchs, C. (2014) *Social Media: A Critical Introduction*. London: SAGE.

Gammage, B. (2008) 'Plain facts: Tasmania under Aboriginal Management'. *Landscape Research* 33(2): 241–54.

Gammage, B. (2011) *The Biggest Estate on Earth: How Aborigines Made Australia*. Crows Nest, NSW: Allen & Unwin.

Gardner, P. D. (2001) *Gippsland Massacres: The Destruction of the Kurnai Tribes, 1800–1860*. Ensay: Ngarak Press.

GBRMPA (2017) 'Reef Health'. *Great Barrier Reef Marine Park Authority* 29 June. Available at: http://www.gbrmpa.gov.au/about-the-reef/reef-health (accessed 13 November 2017).

Geelong Advertiser and Squatters' Advocate (1845) 'Wonderful Discovery of a New Animal'. *Geelong Advertiser and Squatters' Advocate* 2 July. Available at: http://trove.nla.gov.au/newspaper/article/94443733 (accessed 10 November 2017).

Gehman, J., Lefsrud, L. M., and Fast, S. (2017) 'Social License to Operate: Legitimacy by Another Name?'. *Canadian Public Administration* 60(2): 293–317.

Gilmore, D. E. (2002) *Monsters: Evil Beings, Mythical Beasts, and All Manner of Imaginary Terrors*. Philadelphia: University of Pennsylvania Press.

Godfrey-Smith, P. (2016) *Other Minds: The Octopus, the Sea, and the Deep Origins of Consciousness*. New York: Farrar, Straus & Giroux.

Goss, T. (2012) 'A Brief History of Monsters'. *Weird Fiction Review* 15 March. Available at: http://weirdfictionreview.com/2012/03/a-brief-history-of-monsters/ (accessed 11 January 2017).

Gould, C. (1886) *Mythical Monsters*. London: W. H. Allen & Co.

Greenfield, S. (2015) *Mind Change: How Digital Technologies Are Leaving Their Mark on Our Brains*. London: Random House.

Greenberg, H. R. (1986) 'Reimagining the Gargoyle: Psychoanalytic Notes on Alien'. *Camera Obscura: A Journal of Feminism, Culture and Media Studies* 15 (Fall): 86–109.

Greenberg, H. R. (1988) 'Fembo: *Aliens'* Intentions'. *Journal of Popular Film and Television* 15(4): 165–71.

Greenpeace (2014) 'The Trash Vortex'. *Greenpeace*. Available at: http://www.greenpeace.org/international/en/campaigns/oceans/fit-for-the-future/pollution/trash-vortex/ (accessed 7 September 2016).

Grotstein, J. S. (1997) '"Internal Objects" or "Chimerical monsters"? : The Demonic "Third Forms" of the Internal World'. *Journal of Analytical Psychology* 42: 47–80.

Haggarty, N. (2017) 'Scott Morrison Holds a Lump of Coal in Parliament'. *ABC News*, 13 February. Available at: http://www.abc.net.au/news/2017-02-13/scott-morrison-holds-a-lump-of-coal-in-parliament/8264354 (accessed 13 November 2017).

Halberstam, J. (1995) *Skin Shows: Gothic Horror and the Technology of Monsters*. Durham, NC: Duke University Press.

Halilovich, H. (2013) *Places of Pain*. New York: Berghahn.

Halilovich, H. (2016) 'Lessons from Srebrenica: The United Nations after Bosnia'. In: Mayersen, D. (Ed.), *The United Nations and Genocide*. London: Palgrave: 77–100.

Halilovich, H. (2017) *Writing After Srebrenica*. Sarajevo: Buybook.

Halilovich, H. and Phipps, P. (2015) '*Atentat!* Contesting Histories at the One Hundredth Anniversary of the Sarajevo Assassination'. *Journal of Communication, Politics and Culture* 48(3): 29–40.

Hamilton, A. J., R. M. May, and E. K. Waters (2015) 'Here Be Dragons'. *Nature* 520: 42–43.

Hampton, J. (1988) *Hobbes and the Social Contract Tradition.* Cambridge: Cambridge University Press.

Hanich, J. (2011) *Cinematic Emotion in Horror Films and Thrillers: The Aesthetic Paradox of Pleasurable Fear.* Hoboken: Taylor & Francis.

Harker, D. (2003) *Tressell: The Real Story of the Ragged Trousered Philanthropists.* London: Zed Books.

Harpur, P. (1995) *Daimonic Reality: Understanding Otherworldly Encounters.* London: Penguin.

Harvey, D. (1989) *The Condition of Postmodernity: An Enquiry into the Origins of Social Change.* Malden: Blackwell.

Harvey, D. (2001) 'Globalization and the "Spatial Fix"'. *Geographische Revue* 3: 23–30. Available at: http://geographische-revue.de/gr2-01.htm (accessed 1 December 2018).

Harvey, P. (1937) *The Oxford Companion to Classical Literature.* Oxford: Clarendon.

Held, V. (1987) 'Non-Contractual Society: A Feminist View'. *Canadian Journal of Philosophy* 17(1): 111–37.

Held, V. (1993) *Feminist Morality: Transforming Culture, Society, and Politics.* Chicago: University of Chicago Press.

Heller, J. (1961) *Catch-22.* New York: Simon & Schuster.

Hill, S., and Lawrence, S. (2017) *The Atlas of Monsters: Mythical Creatures from Around the World.* London: Big Picture.

Hirsch, E.D, Kett, J.F., and Trefil, J. (Eds.) (2002) *The New Dictionary of Cultural Literacy.* Boston: Houghton Mifflin Company.

Hobbes, T (1651/1904). *Leviathan or The Matter, Forme and Power of a Common Wealth Ecclesiasticall and Civil.* Cambridge: University Press. Open access text available at: https://ia600301.us.archive.org/26/items/leviathanorthem00hobbuoft/leviathanorthem00hobbuoft.pdf (accessed 1 December 2018).

Holden, R., Thomas, D, Green, P. and Holden, N. (2001) *Bunyips: Australia's Folklore of Fear.* Canberra: National Library of Australia.

Holloway, A. (2017) 'Globe on an Ostrich Egg Is World's Oldest Depiction of the New World'. *Ancient Origins* 1 August. Available at: https://goo.gl/PCfgyW (accessed 6 December 2017).

Honig, J., and Both, N. (1997) *Srebrenica: Record of a War Crime.* London: Penguin.

Horsman, R. (1981) *Race and Manifest Destiny*. Cambridge, MA: Harvard University Press.

Hughes, R. (1996) *The Fatal Shore*. London: Harvill.

Humphery-Jenner, M. (2016) 'What Went Wrong with Pokemon Go? Three Lessons from Its Plummeting Player Numbers'. *ABC News* 19 October. Available at: http://www.abc.net.au/news/2016-10-19/what-went-wrong-with-pokemon-go/7942726 (accessed 4 July 2017).

ICTY — International Criminal Tribunal for the former Yugoslavia (2017) Case: Mladić IT-09-92. Available at: http://www.icty.org/case/mladic/4 (accessed on 10 October 2017)

Ingold, T. (2013) 'Dreaming of Dragons: On the Imagination of Real Life'. *The Journal of the Royal Anthropological Institute* 19, 734–52.

Iveson, K. (2016) 'How Pokemon Go Will Make Money from You'. *Sydney Morning Herald* 3 August. Available at: http://www.smh.com.au/comment/how-pokemon-go-will-make-money-from-you-20160802-gqj457.html (accessed 4 July 2017).

Jackson, M. (1995) *At Home in the World*. Durham, NC: Duke University Press.

Jacobson, H. (1970 [1959]) *The First Book of Mythical Beasts*. 2nd, rev. ed. London & New York: Franklin Watts.

Jakica, L. (2010) 'The Problem of Resurrection of Kosovo Mythology in Serbian Popular Culture'. *Transcultural Studies* 6(1): 161–70.

Jansen, T. (2014) 'I Merge Indigenous Stories with My Design—Maybe Others Should too'. *The Conversation*, 14 November. Available at: https://theconversation.com/i-merge-indigenous-stories-with-my-design-maybe-others-should-too-34132 (accessed 10 November 2017).

Jennings, K. (2011) 'Here Be Dragons'. *Slate* 20 September. Available at: http://www.slate.com/articles/health_and_science/science/2011/09/here_be_dragons.html (accessed 5 November 2015)

Jezernik, B. (2004) *Wild Europe: The Balkans in the Gaze of Western Travellers*. London: Saqi.

Jones, D. (2018) *Sleeping with the Lights On: The Unsettling Story of Horror*. Oxford: Oxford University Press.

Kaplan, M. (2013) *The Science of Monsters: The Origins of the Creatures We Love to Fear*. New York: Scribner.

Kaplan, R. (1993) *Balkan Ghosts: A Journey Through History*. New York: Vintage.

Kant, I. (1991) *Kant: Political Writings*. Cambridge: Cambridge University Press.

Kauanui, J. K. (2016) '"A Structure, Not an Event": Settler Colonialism and Enduring Indigeneity'. *Lateral* 5(1). Available at: http://csalateral. org/issue/5-1/forum-alt-humanities-settler-colonialism-enduring-indigeneity-kauanui/ (accessed 25 June 2018)

Keenan, S. (2017) 'Smoke, Curtains and Mirrors: The Production of Race through Time and Title Registration'. *Law and Critique* 28(1), 87–108.

Keil, R., and Mahon, R. (Eds.) (2010) *Leviathan Undone?: Towards a Political Economy of Scale*. Vancouver: UBC Press.

Kelbert, A. W. (2016) 'Climate Change Is a Racist Crisis: That's Why Black Lives Matter Closed an Airport'. *The Guardian* 7 September. Available at: https://www.theguardian.com/commentisfree/2016/sep/06/climate-change-racist-crisis-london-city-airport-black-lives-matter (accessed 7 September 2016).

Kerr, M. (2017) *Scream: Chilling Adventures in the Science of Fear*. New York: Ingram Publisher Services.

Kerr, T. (2003) 'As if Bunyips Mattered... Cross-Cultural Mythopoetic Beasts in Australian Subaltern Planning'. *Journal of Australian Studies* 27 (80): 15–27.

Kingsnorth, P. (2017) *Confessions of a Recovering Environmentalist*. Faber & Faber: London.

Kinnier Wilson, J. V. (1975) 'A Return to the Problems of Behemoth and Leviathan'. *Vetus Testamentum* 25(1): 1–14.

Klein, N. (2014) *This Changes Everything: Capitalism vs. the Climate*. Allen Lane: London.

Kothari, U. (2006) 'An Agenda for Thinking about 'Race' in Development'. *Progress in Development Studies* 6(1): 9–23.

Koudounaris, P. (2016) 'The Monster in the Mirror'. In: Salvesen, B., Shedden, J., and Welch, M. (Eds.), *Guillermo Del Toro: At Home with Monsters – Inside His Films, Notebooks, and Collections*. San Rafael, California: Insight Editions: 43–59.

Krien, A. (2017) 'The Long Goodbye: Coal, Coral and Australia's Climate Deadlock'. *The Quarterly Essay*, 66.

Kumar, R. (1997) *Divide and Fall?: Bosnia in the Annals of Partition*. London: Verso.

Kurspahić, K. (2003) *Prime Time Crime: Balkan Media in War and Peace*. Washington DC: US Institute of Peace Press.

Laffan, M., and Weiss, M. (2012) *Facing Fear: The History of an Emotion in Global Perspective*. Princeton: Princeton University Press.

Lamb, D. S. (1900) 'Mythical Monsters'. *American Anthropologist* (N.S.) 2(2): 277–91.

Landau-Ward, A. (2017) 'Globalization and the Spatial Politics of Cities'. In: Farazmand, A. (Ed.), *Global Encyclopedia of Public Administration, Public Policy, and Governance*. Cham: Springer.

LeBlanc, A. G., and Chaput, J.-P. (2016) 'Pokémon Go: A Game Changer for the Physical Inactivity Crisis?'. *Preventive Medicine* https://doi.org/10.1016/j.ypmed.2016.11.012.

LeDoux, J. (2012) 'Evolution of Human Emotion: A View through Fear'. *Progress in Brain Research* 195: 431–42.

Lee, J. C. H. (2014) "Citizenship and the City: Visions and Revisions of Malaysia". In: Yeoh Seng Guan (Ed.), *The Other Kuala Lumpur: Living in the Shadows of a Globalising Southeast Asian City*. New York: Routledge: 72–91.

Lee, T. B. (2016) 'Pokémon Go Is Everything That Is Wrong with Late Capitalism'. *Vox* 12 July. Available at: https://www.vox.com/2016/7/12/12152728/pokemon-go-economic-problems (accessed 4 July 2017).

Leeming, D. (2005) *The Oxford Companion to World Mythology*. Oxford: Oxford University Press.

Lemanski, M. (2018) 'Plastic on our Plates'. *Weapons of Reason* 5: 76–83.

Le Guin, U. (2014) 'Ursula K Le Guin's Speech at National Book Awards: "Books Aren't just Commodities"'. *The Guardian* 21 November. Available at: https://www.theguardian.com/books/2014/nov/20/ursula-k-le-guin-national-book-awards-speech (accessed 10 June 2018).

Leick, G. (2002 [2001]) *Mesopotamia: The Invention of the City*. Reprint. London: Penguin.

Lévi-Strauss, C. (1966) *The Savage Mind (La Pensée Sauvage)*. London: Weidenfeld & Nicolson.

Litt, T. (2016) *Mutants: Selected Essays*. Kolkata, India: Seagull Books.

Lloyd, S. A., and Sreedhar, S. (2018) 'Hobbes's Moral and Political Philosophy'. In: Zalta, E. N. (Ed.), *The Stanford Encyclopedia of Philosophy* (Summer 2018 Edition). Available at: https://plato.stanford.edu/archives/sum2018/entries/hobbes-moral/ (accessed 2 June 2018).

Locke, J. (1690/2014). In: Cox, R. (Ed.), *Second Treatise of Government: An Essay Concerning the True Original, Extent and End of Civil Government*. Wheeling, IL: Harlan Davidson.

Lovelock, J. (2000) *Gaia: A New Look at Life on Earth*. Oxford: Oxford University Press.

Luck, G. (Ed.) (1987 [1985]) *Arcana Mundi: Magic and the Occult in the Greek and Roman Worlds*. Reprint. London: Crucible.

Lyon, J. (2006) *Kiss of the Butterfly*. Luxembourg: CreateSpace.

Maass, P. (1996) *Love Thy Neighbor: A Story of War*. New York: Random House.

Mabo v. Queensland (No. 2) (1992) 175 Commonwealth Law Reports 1.

McFarlane, A. (2018) 'Thomas Hobbes (1588–1679)', *Philosophy Now* (Brief Lives). Available at: https://philosophynow.org/issues/124/Thomas_Hobbes_1588-1679 (accessed 2 June 2018).

MacFarquhar, N. (2015) 'Russian Movie "Leviathan" Gets Applause in Hollywood but Scorn at Home'. *New York Times* 27 January. Available at: https://www.nytimes.com/2015/01/28/world/europe/leviathan-arussian-movie-gets-applause-in-hollywood-but-scorn-at-home.html (accessed 22 April 2018).

Machiavelli, N. (1961) *The Prince*. London: Penguin.

MacKenzie, L. (1993) *Peacekeeper: The Road to Sarajevo*. Madiera Park, BC: Douglas & McIntyre.

Maier, C. S. (2014) *Leviathan 2.0*. Cambridge, MA: Harvard University Press.

Mair, J. (2002) 'Rewriting the "American Dream": Postmodernism and Otherness in Independence Day". In: Ziaudin, S. and Cubitt, S. (Eds.), *Aliens R Us*. London: Pluto: 34–50.

Maier, S. R., Slovic, P., and Mayorga, M. (2016) 'Reader Reaction to News of Mass Suffering: Assessing the Influence of Story Form and Emotional Response'. *Journalism*, 1–19. DOI: 10.1177/1464884916663597.

Manby, B. (2016) *Shell in Nigeria: Corporate Social Responsibility and the Ogoni Crisis*. Carnegie Council on Ethics & International Affairs. Available at: http://integritynigeria.org/wp-content/uploads/2012/07/Shell-in-Nigeria-Corporate-Social-Responsibility-and-the-Ogoni-Crisis-Bronwen-Manby.pdf. (accessed 9 April 2018).

Manne, R. (2014) 'Wilful Blindness', *The Monthly* December. Available at: https://www.themonthly.com.au/issue/2014/december/1417352400/robert-manne/wilful-blindness (accessed 8 March 2017).

Manne, R. (2015) 'Diabolical: Why Have We Failed to Address Climate Change?'. *The Monthly* December: 24–34.

Marie, T. (2016) 'Seeing the God in Godzilla'. *Comics Alliance* 26 October. Available at: http://comicsalliance.com/my-favorite-monster-godzilla/ (accessed 15 December 2016).

Massey, D. (2007) *World City*. Cambridge: Polity.

McCartney, M. (2016) 'Game on for Pokémon Go'. *BMJ*. doi: 10.1136/bmj. i4306.

McGloin, C., and Georgeou, N. (2015) '"Looks Good on Your CV" The Sociology of Voluntourism Recruitment in Higher Education'. *Journal of Sociology* 52(2): 403–17.

McKinley, B. (2013) 'Kiss of the Butterfly: Review'. Available at: https:// www.vampires.com/review-kiss-of-the-butterfly/ (accessed 5 October 2017).

McKinnell, J. (2014) 'Coal Good for Humanity, Says Abbott'. *The Australian*, 13 October. Available at: https://goo.gl/WQxwPa (accessed 13 November 2017).

McNally, D. (2011) 'Marx's Monsters: Vampire-Capital and the Nightmare-World of Late Capitalism'. In: *Monsters of the Market: Zombies, Vampires and Global Capitalism*. Leiden: Brill: 113–74.

McNally R. T., and Florescu, R. (1994) *In Search of Dracula: The History of Dracula and Vampires*. Boston: Houghton Mifflin Harcourt.

Metzger, J. (2013) 'Raising the Regional Leviathan: A Relational–Materialist Conceptualization of Regions-in-Becoming as Publics-in-Stabilization'. *International Journal of Urban and Regional Research* 37(4): 1368–95.

Meyer, R. (2013) 'No Old Maps Actually Say "Here Be Dragons": But an Ancient Globe Does'. *The Atlantic* 12 December. Available at: http:// www.theatlantic.com/technology/archive/2013/12/no-old-maps-actually-say-here-be-dragons/282267/ (accessed 31 August 2016).

Midgley, M. (2011) *The Myths We Live By*. New York & London: Routledge.

Mignolo, W. (2011) *The Darker Side of Western Modernity: Global Futures, Decolonial Options*. Durham, NC: Duke University Press: 1–26.

Milburn, C. N. (2003) 'Monsters in Eden: Darwin and Derrida'. *Modern Language Notes* 118(3): 603–21.

Miller, C. (1974) *A Dictionary of Monsters and Mysterious Beasts*. London & Sydney: Pan.

Milman, O. (2016) '"Great Pacific Garbage Patch" Far Bigger than Imagined, Aerial Survey Shows'. *Guardian* 5 October. Available at: https://www. theguardian.com/environment/2016/oct/04/great-pacific-garbage-patch-ocean-plastic-trash (accessed 4 October 2016).

Mills, C. W. (1997) *The Racial Contract*. Ithaca: Cornell University Press.

Mittman, A. S. (2016 [2012]) 'Introduction: The Impact of Monsters and Monster Studies'. In: Mittman, A. S. and Dendle, P. J. (Eds.), *The*

Ashgate Research Companion to Monsters and the Monstrous. London: Routledge: 1–14.

Mode, H. (1973) *Fabulous Beasts and Demons*. London: Phaidon.

Moffat, K., and Zhang, A. (2014) 'The Paths to Social Licence to Operate: An Integrative Model Explaining Community Acceptance of Mining'. *Resources Policy* 39: 61–70.

Moffitt, J. F., and Sebastián, S. (1996) *O Brave New People: The European Invention of the American Indian*. Albuquerque: University of New Mexico Press.

Moloney, P. (2011) 'Hobbes, Savagery, and International Anarchy'. *American Political Science Review* 105(1): 189–204.

Moore, R. (2017) 'The Grenfell Tragedy Exposes a Tawdry Culture That Has Held Sway for Too Long'. *The Guardian* 18 June. https://www.theguardian.com/commentisfree/2017/jun/17/grenfell-tower-tragedy-exposes-tawdry-culture (accessed 8 July 2017).

Moreton-Robinson, A. (2007) *Sovereign Subjects: Indigenous Sovereignty Matters*. Crows Nest, NSW: Allen & Unwin.

Moreton-Robinson, A. (2015) *The White Possessive: Property, Power and Indigenous Sovereignty*. Minneapolis: University of Minnesota Press.

Mulhall, S. (2002) *On Film*. New York: Routledge.

Nasr, S. V. R. (2001) *Islamic Leviathan: Islam and the Making of State Power*. Oxford: Oxford University Press.

Ness, P. (2012 [2011]) *A Monster Calls*. Reprint. London: Walker Books.

Newsom, C. A. (2009) *The Book of Job: A Contest of Moral Imaginations*. Oxford: Oxford University Press.

Nietzsche, F. (1989 [1967]) *On the Genealogy of Morals* and *Ecce Homo*. Kaufmann, W. (Trans.). Reprint. New York: Vintage Books/Random House.

Nietzsche, F. W. (1995) *Thus Spoke Zarathustra*. New York: Modern Library.

Noble, L. (2011) *Medicinal Cannibalism in Early Modern English Literature and Culture*. New York: Palgrave Macmillan.

Nuhanović, H. (2007) *Under the UN Flag: The International Community and the Srebrenica Genocide*. Sarajevo: DES.

O'Donnell, T. (2014) 'Here's Why I'm a Proud Godzilla Supporter'. *The New Yorker* 14 April. Available at: http://www.newyorker.com/humor/daily-shouts/heres-why-im-a-proud-godzilla-supporter (accessed 7 September 2016).

Ó Donghaile, D. (2018) 'Modernism, Class and Colonialism in Robert Noonan's *The Ragged Trousered Philanthropists*'. *Irish Studies Review*: 1–16.

Ogilvie, R. M. (2000 [1969]) *The Romans and their Gods*. Reprint. London: Pimlico.

Orthia, L. A. (2010) '"Sociopathetic Abscess" or "Yawning Chasm"? The Absent Postcolonial Transition in Doctor Who'. *Journal of Commonwealth Literature* 45(2): 207–25.

Ortner, S. B. (1974) 'Is Female to Male as Nature Is to Culture?'. In: Rosaldo, M. Z. and Lamphere, L. (Eds.), *Woman, Culture, and Society*. Stanford: Stanford University Press: 67–87.

O'Shaughnessy, P. T. (2008) 'Parachuting Cats and Crushed Eggs: The Controversy Over the Use of DDT to Control Malaria'. *American Journal of Public Health* 98(11): 1940–48.

Otto, K. (2005) *Yarra: A Diverting History of Melbourne's Murky River*. Melbourne: Text Publishing.

Owen, J. R., and Kemp, D. (2013) 'Social Licence and Mining: A Critical Perspective'. *Resources Policy* 38(1): 29–35.

Pahuja, S. (2011) *Decolonising International Law: Development, Economic Growth and the Politics of Universality*. Cambridge: Cambridge University Press.

Park, K., and Daston, L. (1981) 'Unnatural Conceptions: The Study of Monsters in Sixteenth-and Seventeenth-Century France and England', *Past and Present* 92 (August): 20–54.

Pascoe, B. (2015) *Dark Emu, Black Seeds: Agriculture or Accident*. Broome: Magabala.

Pateman, C. (1989) *The Sexual Contract*. Stanford: Stanford University Press.

Pateman C., and Mills, C. (2007) *Contract and Domination*. Stanford: Polity.

Perić, B., and Pletenac, T. (2015) *Land beyond the Forest. Vampire Myth in Literature and Film*. Zagreb: Tim Press.

Perlman, F. (1983) *Against His-story, against Leviathan!*. Detroit: Black & Red.

Phillipp, B. (2016) 'Origins of 10 of the Most Iconic Monsters from Pop Culture'. *The Chive* 28 October. Available at: http://thechive.com/2016/10/28/the-origins-of-10-of-the-most-iconic-monsters-from-pop-culture-10-photos/ (accessed 9 July 2017).

Platt, P. G. (Ed.) (1999) *Wonders, Marvels, and Monsters in Early Modern Culture*. Newark: University of Delaware Press.

Porter, L. (2018) 'From an Urban Country to Urban Country: Confronting the Cult of Denial in Australian Cities'. *Australian Geographer* 49(2): 239–46.

Prasad, A. (2015) 'Teratomas: The Tumours That Can Transform into "Evil Twins"'. *The Guardian* 27 April. Available at: https://www.theguardian. com/commentisfree/2015/apr/27/teratoma-tumour-evil-twin-cancer (accessed 4 July 2017).

Pratt, J. W. (1927) 'The Origin of "Manifest Destiny"'. *The American Historical Review* 32(4): 795–98.

Prno, J., and Slocombe, D. S. (2012) 'Exploring the Origins of "Social License to Operate" in the Mining Sector: Perspectives from Governance and Sustainability Theories'. *Resources policy* 37(3): 346–57.

Quammen, D. (2003) *Monster of God: The Man-Eating Predator in the Jungles of History and the Mind*. New York: W. W. Norton.

Rappaport, R. A. (1999) *Ritual and Religion in the Making of Humanity*. Cambridge: Cambridge University Press.

Ratnesar, R. (2001) 'The Hunt for Osama bin Laden'. *Time* 18 November. Available at: http://content.time.com/time/magazine/ article/0,9171,1001287,00.html (accessed on 14 September 2016)

Ravilious, K. (2017) 'When Two Disasters Saved Earth from a Worse One'. *Guardian* 4 September. Available at: https://www.theguardian. com/science/2017/sep/03/pinatubo-volcano-typhoon-ozone-layer- terrawatch (accessed 6 September 2017).

Read, P. (2000) *Belonging: Australians, Place and Aboriginal Ownership*. Cambridge: Cambridge University Press.

Readfern, G. (2018) 'Earth's Climate Monsters Could Be Unleashed as Temperatures Rise', *Guardian* 6 October. Available at: https://www. theguardian.com/environment/planet-oz/2018/oct/06/earths- climate-monsters-could-be-unleashed-as-temperatures-rise (accessed 9 October 2018).

RN (2015) 'The Future of the Enlightenment'. *Big Ideas* 3 November. Available at: http://www.abc.net.au/radionational/programs/bigideas/21st- century-enlightenment/6874064 (accessed 11 November 2015).

Robbins, M. (2014) 'Mind Change: Susan Greenfield Has a Big Idea, but What Is It?'. *The Guardian* 3 October. Available at: https://www.theguardian. com/science/the-lay-scientist/2014/oct/03/mind-change-susan- greenfield-has-a-big-idea-but-what-is-it (accessed 4 July 2017).

Robbins, N. W. (2014) 'Civilization of the Living Dead: Canonical Monstrosity, the Romero Zombie, and the Political Subject'. *CUNY Academic Works.* Available at: https://academicworks.cuny.edu/gc_etds/468 (accessed 1 December 2018).

Robinson, F. N. (Ed.) (1957) *The Works of Geoffrey Chaucer.* 2nd ed. Oxford: Oxford University Press.

Roddy, M. (2014) 'Russia's "Leviathan" Pleases Cannes, Angers Russian Minister'. *Reuters Entertainment News* 24 May. Available at: https://www.reuters.com/article/us-filmfestival-cannes-russia/russias-leviathan-pleases-cannes-angers-russian-minister-idUSKBN0E31HM20140523 (accessed 22 April 2018).

Romanin, L. M., Hopf, F., Haberle, S. G., and Bowman, D. M. (2016) 'Fire Regime and Vegetation Change in the Transition from Aboriginal to European Land Management in a Tasmanian Eucalypt Savanna'. *Australian Journal of Botany* 64(5): 427–40.

Rose, D. B. (1996) *Nourishing Terrains: Australian Aboriginal Views of Landscape and Wilderness.* Canberra: Australian Heritage Commission.

Rowse, T. (2001) 'Terra nullius'. In: Davison, G., Hirst, J., and Macintyre, S. (Eds.) *The Oxford Companion to Australian History.* Oxford: Oxford University Press.

RT News (2015) '"Hollywood, Orthodox-Style": Church Activists Want Golden Globe-winning film "Leviathan" Banned'. *RT News* 15 January. Available at: https://www.rt.com/news/222987-hollywood-orthodox-leviathan-ban/ (accessed 22 April 2018).

Ryall, J. (2016) 'Sentence in Japan's first Pokemon Go Death Criticised as Too Lenient'. *The Telegraph* 11 November. Available at: http://www.telegraph.co.uk/news/2016/11/01/sentence-in-japans-first-pokemon-go-death-criticised-as-too-leni/ (accessed 4 July 2017).

Ryan, L. (1996) *The Aboriginal Tasmanians.* St Leonards, NSW: Allen & Unwin.

Sagan, C. (1978) *Dragons of Eden: Speculations on the Evolution of Human Intelligence.* London: Book Club Associates.

Said, E. W. (1995) *Orientalism: Western Conceptions of the Orient.* London: Penguin.

Said. E. W. (2004) *Power, Politics, and Culture: Interviews with Edward W. Said.* London: Bloomsbury.

Sassen, S. (2008) *Territory, Authority, Rights: From Medieval to Global Assemblages.* Princeton, NJ: Princeton University Press.

Seldon, S., and Lee, J. C. H. (2016) 'On the Origins of Culture and Change: Stochastic Processes in Malaysia and South Africa'. In: Lee, J. C. H., Prior, J. M. and Reuter, T. (Eds.), *Trajectories: Excursions with the Work of E. Douglas Lewis*. New York: Peter Lang: 233–50.

Self, W. (2011) 'The Arms Trade'. *A Point of View* 30 October. Available at: http://www.bbc.co.uk/programmes/b01694p0 (accessed 8 July 2017).

Self, W. (2016) 'Self's Search for Meaning: Science'. *BBC* 8 August 2016. Available at: http://www.bbc.co.uk/programmes/b07dknm1 (accessed 2 July 2017).

Self, W. (2017) 'After Grenfell'. *A Point of View* 25 June. Available at: http://www.bbc.co.uk/programmes/b08v8vh0 (accessed 8 July 2017).

shiomiga1djura (2011) 'Ratko Mladic Srebrenica'. *YouTube*, 11 January. Available at: https://www.youtube.com/watch?v=lX5An6jpUKs (accessed 27 October 2017).

Sells, M. (1996) *The Bridge Betrayed: Religion and Genocide in Bosnia*. Berkeley: University of California Press.

Sharon, T., and Woolley, J. D. (2004) 'Do Monsters Dream? Young Children's Understanding of the Fantasy/Reality Distinction'. *British Journal of Developmental Psychology* 22: 293–310.

Shukar, K. (1996) *In Search of Prehistoric Survivors: Do Giant 'Extinct' Creatures Still Exist?*. London: Blandford.

Slack, K. (2008) *Corporate Social License and Community Consent: Policy Innovations*. Carnegie Council. Available at: https://www.carnegiecouncil.org/publications/archive/policy_innovations/commentary/000094 (accessed 10 April 2018).

Slater, S. (2014) 'Monsters of the Mind: Is There a Perceptual Basis for the Darkness that Lurks within?'. *Psychology Today* February 28. Available at: https://www.psychologytoday.com/blog/the-dolphin-divide/201402/monsters-the-mind (accessed 6 July 2017).

Sontag, S. (1965) 'The Imagination of Disaster'. *Commentary* 1 October. Available at: http://www.commentarymagazine.com/articles/the-imagination-of-disaster/ (accessed 15 October 2017).

South Africa History Online (2018) 'Cecil John Rhodes' entry. Available at: www.sahistory.org.za/people/cecil-john-rhodes8 (accessed 25 June 2018).

Spivak, G. (1999) *A Critique of Postcolonial Reason: Toward a History of the Vanishing Present*. Cambridge, MA: Harvard University Press.

Steger, M. B., and Wilson, E. K. (2012) 'Anti-Globalization or Alter-Globalization? Mapping the Political Ideology of the Global Justice Movement'. *International Studies Quarterly* 56(3): 439–54.

Steven, M. (2017) *Splatter Capital: The Political Economy of Gore Films*. London: Repeater.

Stevens, A. (1999 [1998]) 'Monsters and Fabulous Beasts'. In: *Ariadne's Clue: A Guide to the Symbols of Humankind*. Princeton, NJ: Princeton University Press: 367–78.

Stillman, R. E. (1995a) 'Hobbes's "Leviathan": Monsters, Metaphors, and Magic'. *English Literary History* 62(4), 791–819.

Stillman, R. E. (1995b) *The New Philosophy and Universal Languages in Seventeenth-Century England: Bacon, Hobbes, and Wilkins*. Lewisburg: Bucknell University Press.

Stokoe, J. et al. (2016) *Godzilla in Hell*. San Diego: IDW.

Strauss, L. (1936/1963) *The Political Philosophy of Hobbes: Its Basis and Its Genesis*. Chicago: University of Chicago Press.

Sutcliffe, R. J. (2011) 'The Imaginary Excess of Reason: Critical Reflections on Magic and Modernity in the Context of Post-Millennial Capitalism'. In: Patterson, M., and Macintyre, M. (Eds.), *Managing Modernity in the Western Pacific*. St Lucia: University of Queensland Press: 30–58.

Sugg, R. (2011) *Mummies, Cannibals and Vampires: The History of Corpse Medicine from the Renaissance to the Victorians*. London: Routledge.

Tacitus, P. C. (1986) *The Annals* and *The Histories*. Church, A. J., and Brodribb, W. J. (Trans.). Chicago: William Benton.

Tatz, C. (1999) 'Genocide in Australia'. *Journal of Genocide Research* 1(3): 315–52.

Time (2017) 'Bosnia: Ron Haviv 1992'. *Time* Available at: http://100photos. time.com/photos/ron-haviv-bosnia (accessed on 1 October 2017).

Thomas, K. (1987 [1983]) *Man and the Natural World: Changing Attitudes in England 1500–1800*. Reprint. Harmondsworth: Penguin.

Tressell, R. (1914/2018) *The Ragged Trousered Philanthropists*. Frankfurt: Outlook Verlag.

Tsing, A. L., Swanson, H. A., Gan, E., and Bubandt, N. (2017a) 'Introduction: Bodies Tumbling into Bodies'. In: Tsing, A. L., et al. (Eds.), *Arts of Living on a Damaged Planet: Monsters of the Anthropocene*. Minneapolis: University of Minnesota Press: M1-M12.

Tsing, A. L., Swanson, H. A., Gan, E., and Bubandt, N. (Eds.) (2017b) *Arts of Living on a Damaged Planet: Ghosts/Monsters of the Anthropocene*. Minneapolis: University of Minnesota Press.

Tsutsui, W. (2004) *Godzilla: Fifty Years of the King of the Monsters*. New York: Palgrave.

Tsutsui, W. (2014) 'For Godzilla and Country'. *Foreign Affairs* 27 May. Available at: https://www.foreignaffairs.com/articles/united-states/2014-05-27/godzilla-and-country (accessed 8 March 2017).

Turner, B. S., and Khondker, H. H. (2010) *Globalization East and West*. London: SAGE.

Ulstein, G. (2017) 'Brave New Weird: Anthropocene Monsters in Jeff VanderMeer's *The Southern Reach*'. *Concentric: Literary and Cultural Studies* 43(1): 71–96.

Uongozi Institute (2018) 'Interview with: Canadian Ambassador to Tanzania and President of McAlister Consulting Corporation, Amb. Andrew McAlister'. *In Focus*, published on 9 January 2018. Available at: <https://www.youtube.com/watch?v=nOyWfyVKnBo> (accessed 15 January 2018).

Vassilieva, J. (2018) 'Russian Leviathan: Power, Landscape, Memory'. *Film Criticism* 42(1).

Viveiros de Castro, E. (2014) *Cannibal Metaphysics*. Minneapolis: Univocal.

Vrbančić, M. S. Božić, and Vrbančić, S. (2011) 'Different Adaptations: The Power of the Vampire', [*Sic*] časopis za književnost, kulturu i književno prevođenje. DOI: 10.15291/SIC/2.1.LC.4.

Wacquant, L. (2010) 'Crafting the Neoliberal State: Workfare, Prisonfare, and Social Insecurity'. *Sociological Forum* 25(2): 197–220.

Wagner, J. (1973) *The Bunyip of Berkeley's Creek*, pictures by Ron Brooks. Ringwood: Puffin.

Waldron, J. (1990) *The Right to Private Property*. Oxford: Clarendon Press.

Walker, S. (2014) 'Leviathan Director Andrei Zvyagintsev: "Living in Russia Is Like Being in a Minefield"'. *The Guardian* 14 November. Available at: https://www.theguardian.com/film/2014/nov/06/leviathan-director-andrei-zvyagintsev-russia-oscar-contender-film (accessed 25 April 2018).

Wanhalla, A. (2010) 'The Politics of "Periodical Counting": Race, Place and Identity in Southern New Zealand'. In: Mar, T. B., Edmonds, P. (Eds.), *Making Settler Colonial Space: Perspectives on Race, Place and Identity*. London: Palgrave Macmillan: 198–217.

Warner, M. (2007) *Monsters of Our Own Making: The Peculiar Pleasures of Fear*. Lexington: University Press of Kentucky.

Watson, I. (2000) 'Talking up Aboriginal Law in a Sea of Genocide' (Interview with Robbie Thorpe) *Indigenous Law Bulletin* 5(1): 14.

Watson, I. (2002) *Looking at You, Looking at Me...Aboriginal Culture and History of the South-east of South Australia*. Adelaide: University of South Australia.

Watson, I. (2009) 'Sovereign Spaces, Caring for Country, and the Homeless Position of Aboriginal Peoples'. *South Atlantic Quarterly* 108(1): 27–51.

Watson, D. (1984) *Caledonia Australis: Scottish Highlanders on the Frontier of Australia*. Sydney: Collins.

Watts, R. (2008) 'Making Numbers Count: The Birth of the Census and Racial Government in Victoria, 1835–1840'. *Australian Historical Studies* 34(121): 26–47.

Weiss, A. S. (2004) 'Ten Theses on Monsters and Monstrosity'. *The Drama Review* 48(1): 124–25.

West, R. (1941) *Black Lamb and Grey Falcon: A Journey through Yugoslavia*. London: Macmillan.

Wild, M. (2012) 'Global Dimming and Brightening'. *Bulletin of the American Meteorological Society* 93(1): 27–37.

Winship, M. (2016) 'Naomi Klein: "There Are No Non-Radical Options Left Before Us". *Salon* 5 February. Available at: http://www.salon.com/2016/02/04/naomi_klein_there_are_no_non_radical_options_left_before_us_partner/ (accessed 8 March 2017).

Wittgenstein, L. (1979) *Remarks on Frazer's Golden Bough*. Rhees, R. (Ed.), Miles, A. C. (Trans.). Retford: Brynmill.

Wittgower, R. (1942) 'Marvels of the East: A Study in the History of Monsters'. *Journal of the Warburg and Courtauld Institutes* 5: 159–97.

Wolfe, P. (2006) 'Settler Colonialism and the Elimination of the Native'. *Journal of Genocide Research* 8(4): 387–409.

Wolff, L. (1994) *Inventing Eastern Europe. The Map of Civilization on the Mind of the Enlightenment*. Stanford: Stanford University Press.

Yeoh, B. S. (2005) 'The Global Cultural City? Spatial Imagineering and Politics in the (multi) Cultural Marketplaces of South-East Asia'. *Urban Studies* 42(5–6): 945–58.

Žižek, S. (1991) 'Grimaces of the Real, or When the Phallus Appears'. *October* 58: 44–68.

Žižek, S. (2016) *Disparities*. London: Bloomsbury Academic.

350.ORG (2017) 'Raise a Paddle: A Journey from the Pacific Islands to the Tar Sands'. *350.ORG* 5 June. Available at: https://www.youtube.com/watch?v=YqXm23e1ZRE (accessed 10 June 2017).

About the Authors

Julian C. H. Lee is a Associate Professor of Global Studies, in the School of Global, Urban and Social Studies, RMIT University, where he is also associated with the Social and Global Studies Centre. His anthropological research has focused on civil society, gender, sexuality and multiculturalism in Malaysia, Indonesia and Australia. His published academic work includes his sole-authored books *Second Thoughts: On Malaysia, Globalisation, Society and Self*; *Women's Activism in Malaysia*; and *Policing Sexuality: Sex, Society, and the State*. He is also the editor of *Narratives of Globalization*, and *The Malaysian Way of Life*, and co-editor with Yeoh Seng Guan of *Fringe Benefits*, with Marco Ferrarese of *Authenticity in Thailand, Indonesia and Malaysia*, and with John Prior and Thomas Reuter of *Trajectories: Excursions with the Anthropology of E. Douglas Lewis*. His short non-fiction films include 'For Japan, Our Sister', 'Be a Superhero' and 'Caring at a Distance'.

Hariz Halilovich is an award-winning social anthropologist and author; he is Associate Professor and Vice-Chancellor's Senior Research Fellow at the Social and Global Studies Centre, RMIT University, Melbourne. His main research areas include place-based identity politics, forced migration, politically motivated violence, memory studies and human rights. Much of his work has an applied focus, and he has conducted research on migration and human rights-related issues for a range of non-governmental and governmental bodies, including the Minister for Immigration and Citizenship (Australia). His award-winning book *Places of Pain: Forced Displacement, Popular Memory and Trans-local Identities in Bosnian War–torn Communities* was published by Berghahn, New York–Oxford and his latest book *Writing After Srebrenica* by Buybook, Sarajevo. In addition to academic text-based outputs, he has also produced multimedia exhibitions, works of fiction and radio and TV programs.

Ani Landau-Ward is associated with the Social and Global Studies Centre and the Centre for Urban Research at RMIT University, where she has been teaching international development, social and political theory, and globalisation in RMIT's Bachelor of Arts (International Studies) program. Her current PhD research is a socio-legal analysis of the governance and justice implications of digitisation in property rights administration, in the international law and development field. She brings to her academic work professional experience in community work, land and housing justice advocacy, and participatory architectural design. Her research has been presented at the annual meetings of The Association for Law Property and Society, and the International Academic Association on Planning, Law, and Property Rights. She has also published on the opportunities for Indigenous land governance with the Centre for Urban Research. Her scholarly writing has been published in the *Springer Global Encyclopedia of Public Administration, Public Policy, and Governance*; the *New Zealand Journal of Asian Studies*, and the volume *Urban Asias: Essays on Futurity Past and Present*.

Peter Phipps is a Senior Lecturer in Global Studies at RMIT University, where he is also associated with the Social and Global Studies Centre. He undertook post-graduate training in cultural anthropology at the University of California Berkeley, and completed a PhD on the cultural politics of postcolonial theory at the University of Melbourne. He has published in journals including *Ethnos*, *Alternatives*, and *Communication, Politics and Culture* on Indigenous festivals, commemorations, tourism and the politics of cultural globalization. He is a founding member of the Centre for Global Research and has consulted to a number of organizations and government bodies including the City of Melbourne, Victorian Multicultural Commission, the PNG Department for Community Development, ATSIC, ATSIAB (Australia Council), UNDP (Sarajevo) and the Yothu Yindi Foundation.

Richard J. Sutcliffe is an independent researcher who has conducted research on new religious movements and urban youth culture. He is interested in the role of the creative imagination in the articulation of human social life and the inter-urban dynamics of emergent forms of transnational visual culture. He has written on subjects including Western esotericism, social theories of modernity, globalization, and street art. His writing has been published in places including the journal *Canberra Anthropology*, and in the volumes *Paganism Today, Managing Modernity in the Western Pacific, The Malaysian Way of Life, Second Thoughts: On Malaysia, Globalisation, Society and Self*, and the Springer *Global Encyclopedia of Public Administration, Public Policy, and Governance*.

Credits

Cover created by Kısmet Press from: 1) 'Broached Monsters, Pankalangu Armchair', designed by Trent Jansen, produced by J.P. Finsbury, Sydney, photographed by Michael Corridore. © J.P. Finsbury and Michael Corridore. Reproduced with permission; 2 'The sleep of reason produces monsters (El sueño de la razon produce monstruos)', by Francisco de Goya y Lucientes. <https://www.metmuseum.org/art/collection/search/338473>; 3) figure of a Bunyip skull, from *The Tasmanian Journal of Natural Science*, January 1847 <https://commons.wikimedia.org/wiki/File:Bunyip_skull.jpg>; 4) starling murmuration, photo taken at RSPB Minsmere in 2015 (22224627666) (Licence: CC BY-SA 2.0); 5) engraving of Charles La Trobe <https://commons.wikimedia.org/wiki/File:Charleslatrobe.jpg>. Images 2, 3, and 5 in the public domain. Images 1–3 in public domain. All images edited by Kısmet Press, and republished under their original licence.

Frontispiece created by Kısmet Press from: 1) 'The sleep of reason produces monsters (El sueño de la razon produce monstruos)', by Francisco de Goya y Lucientes. <https://www.metmuseum.org/art/collection/search/338473>; 2) figure of a Bunyip skull, from *The Tasmanian Journal of Natural Science*, January 1847 <https://commons.wikimedia.org/wiki/File:Bunyip_skull.jpg>; 3) Destruction of Leviathan, 1865 engraving by Gustave Doré <https://en.wikipedia.org/wiki/File:Destruction_of_Leviathan.png>; 4) starling murmuration, photo taken at RSPB Minsmere in 2015 (22224627666) (Licence: CC BY-SA 2.0); 5) State Library of Victoria La Trobe Reading room (photo by David Iliff. Licence: CC-BY-SA 3.0) <https://commons.wikimedia.org/wiki/File:State_Library_of_Victoria_La_Trobe_Reading_room_5th_floor_view.jpg>. Images 1–3 in public domain. All images edited by Kısmet Press, and republished under their original licence.

Endorsements

This volume offers an exciting and innovative reflection on the current anxieties, challenges and dangers of our current global era by inviting us to 'think through monsters'. This invocation points to looming unknowns, shape-shifting ambiguities, and decentering logics of fear and possibility which together facilitate new modes of intimate engagement with a range of issues such as colonial violence, environmental degradation, decline of the west, and the enduring pain of genocide. This is a beautiful, moving, timely and evocative collection.

> — Eve Darian-Smith, Chair, Department of Global and International Studies, University of California Irvine, and co-author of *The Global Turn* and author of *Laws and Societies in Global Contexts.*

This insightful and powerful book challenges us to learn from our monsters about ourselves and our past, and to face our increasingly uncertain future alongside them.

> — Liz Gloyn, Senior Lecturer in Classics, Royal Holloway, University of London, and author of *Tracking Classical Monsters in Popular Culture* and *The Ethics of the Family in Seneca.*

Monsters may be as old as human life (and our collective anxieties) and today they continue to stalk us — and fascinate us — in a time of technological transformation, inexorable globalisation, and political polarisation. Investigating the creatures of contemporary popular culture as well as less-celebrated beasts from Australian folklore to war crimes tribunals, *Monsters of Modernity* explores our anxieties and obsessions through the monstrous imaginary of dark colonial legacies, the profound consequences of global warming, and the pervasive influence of state power and capitalism. Like monsters themselves, this volume is unconstrained and fearless, ranging across geographies and chronologies, breaking through traditional disciplinary boundaries, and challenging the conventions of staid academic writing. *Monsters of Modernity* is a sophisticated, imaginative, provocative, and very welcome addition to the growing scholarly literature on the significance of our deep and enduring need for monsters.

— William M. Tsutsui, President and Professor of History, Hendrix College, and author of *Godzilla on My Mind* and *Japanese Popular Culture and Globalization*.

Monsters of Modernity explores the contemporary human condition through a selection of globally iconic monsters. In each chapter, the authors explore monsters for what they reveal about the world in which we live and for the ways that they enable us to address critical issues facing humanity. Although monsters might be feared and thought of as threatening, the authors show how each monster brings us to a deeper appreciation of various aspects of our troubled world, from gender relations, to the lasting impacts of colonisation, to neoliberalism, to the fragility of humanity's place in the world in the Anthropocene.

Monsters of Modernity explores new ground in the conventions of authorship and scholarship. This book will be a valuable companion to anyone interested in the study of monsters as well as those seeking engaging ways to explore and teach key global issues.

Join the authors as they explore the critical condition of our age through their explorations of Chimera, Leviathan, Vampires, Bunyips, Predator and the Xenomorph Alien, Pokémon, Dragons, and Godzilla.

Kismet Press is a not-for-profit partnership committed to publishing high-quality, peer-reviewed works in the arts and humanities, and making them as accessible as possible, both in print and open access online.

The authors have foregone their royalty rights to make this book free to read online and to download via the publisher's website.

kısmet·press

Libera Scientia | Free Knowledge

www.ingramcontent.com/pod-product-compliance
Lightning Source LLC
Chambersburg PA
CBHW070930030426
42336CB00014BA/2615